"Rooted in the conviction that God's purposes unfold in our neighborhoods, Amar Peterman calls readers to focus close to home, reminding us that faithful citizenship begins with knowing and serving our neighbors, especially across lines of difference, and that the common good is cultivated through incarnate engagement that reflects God's care for the world."

—**Stephanie Summers,** CEO of The Center for Public Justice

"If meals make neighbors, and neighbors make communities, then the table is far more than a place to eat. In *Becoming Neighbors*, Amar Peterman reminds us that the table is where we learn to linger, to see and be seen, and to be knit together—often against the grain of an age bent toward isolation, suspicion, and speed. Hospitality here is no small courtesy; it is a school of hope, where imagination is reawakened and the quiet miracle of God's presence can still break in."

—**Anne Snyder,** editor in chief, *Comment*

"Amar Peterman blends clarity, compassion, and depth in his call for Christians to take seriously the kind of generous hospitality that is possible at the intersection of faithful witness and love of neighbor. Reading this book is time well spent."

—**John Inazu,** author of *Learning to Disagree: The Surprising Path to Navigating Differences with Empathy and Respect*

"In a digital age in which the entire world seems like our neighborhood, it is easy to overlook our own local, flesh-and-blood, brick-and-mortar communities. It is easy to want to change the whole world but not even know our own neighbors. Amar Peterman invites us to turn more toward the places where we dwell, to the people who live among us, and to the spaces where we can cultivate the common good in our own communities—in other words, to become more neighborly. Loving our neighbors with Christlike love is a process of our own becoming, and I'm grateful that upon reading these pages, I'm inspired and encouraged to participate more fully in that process of becoming."

—**Karen Swallow Prior,** author of *You Have a Calling: Finding Your Vocation in the True, Good, and Beautiful*

"Amar Peterman connects cosmic beliefs to concrete actions in this beautiful book about how faith calls us to build community, starting with the people who live next door."

—**Eboo Patel,** author of *We Need to Build: Field Notes for Diverse Democracy*

"As Christians we are called to become neighbors—and that is not a metaphor! Amar Peterman's reminder that love must be concrete is as invitational as it is insistent, and as visionary as it is provocatively practical."

—**Hanna Reichel,** author of *For Such a Time as This: An Emergency Devotional*

"Amar Peterman brings to the American church the ancient, precolonial values of peaceful pluralism embodied by our Indian ancestors, values the West desperately needs for its healing today. This book is a hope-filled, prophetic reimagination of what the church was always meant to be—good news for the poor and oppressed, working alongside the Spirit of God who is already present in all of humanity and creation. If you're longing for a church that heals, hopes, and joins God's liberating work in the world, read this book."

—**Joash P. Thomas,** author of *The Justice of Jesus: Reimagining Your Church's Life Together to Pursue Liberation and Wholeness*

"Amar Peterman has written a book the church desperately needs. *Becoming Neighbors* is a beautiful vision of what happens when we move past fear and suspicion and begin to see one another as bearers of God's image. It's both deeply practical and profoundly hopeful—an invitation to create communities marked by love, justice, and belonging."

—**Zach W. Lambert,** author of *Better Ways to Read the Bible: Transforming a Weapon of Harm into a Tool of Healing*

BECOMING NEIGHBORS

The Common Good Made Local

Amar D. Peterman

William B. Eerdmans Publishing Company
Grand Rapids, Michigan

Wm. B. Eerdmans Publishing Co.
2006 44th Street SE, Grand Rapids, MI 49508
www.eerdmans.com

Published 2026
Printed in the United States of America

32 31 30 29 28 27 26 1 2 3 4 5 6 7

ISBN 978-0-8028-8412-1

Library of Congress Cataloging-in-Publication Data

Names: Peterman, Amar D., 1996– author
Title: Becoming neighbors : the common good made local / Amar D. Peterman.
Description: Grand Rapids, Michigan : William B. Eerdmans Publishing Company, [2026] | Includes bibliographical references and index. | Summary: "The author explores how communities can be transformed through the Christian practice of neighbor love and a theologically informed understanding of the common good"—Provided by publisher.
Identifiers: LCCN 2025021187 | ISBN 9780802884121 paperback | ISBN 9781467468244 epub
Subjects: LCSH: Love—Religious aspects—Christianity—Meditations | Neighbors—Miscellanea | Meditations | LCGFT: Meditations
Classification: LCC BV4639 .P473 2026 | DDC 241/.4—dc23/eng/20250925
LC record available at https://lccn.loc.gov/2025021187

To Ashish:

A light in the darkness. A blessing to the world.

Dhanyavad, Varma ji.

CONTENTS

FOREWORD

Beginning several years ago, I started to notice how often Amar Peterman's contributions in places like *Sojourners* and *Christian Century* arrested my attention and provoked my thinking. His cultural commentary and theological reflection wed sharp intelligence with pastoral sensitivity. Rather than merely offering observations from a safe distance, here was theology that offered a hand. Here was a writer attuned to contemporary challenges who, in refreshing ways, refused to pen the sorts of ideological screeds that always feel predictable. While his peers were offering "hot takes" that felt immediately tired, Peterman was inviting us to reflection and practice with a further horizon in view. This was someone who was seeking wisdom and offering care.

This potent little book embodies all of this.

I am tempted to say that Amar writes "from the trenches" as a practitioner and organizer (serving as Assistant Director of Civic Networks for Interfaith America). But that would be the wrong metaphor, since Amar endeavors to liberate us from the culture wars. He invites us to climb out of our various entrenched positions and, instead, come sit together at a table where we can learn to be neighbors again. So perhaps it's better to say that Amar, the practitioner-theologian and scholar-activist, writes "from the kitchen," as it were—as someone with real, incarnate experience of organizing potlucks that bring together an array of dishes as diverse and wondrous as the population of the USA. This book dreams of this as an allegory for our neighborhoods and nation.

Amar echoes Eboo Patel in describing the United States as "a potluck nation." There is something wonderfully wild about a potluck dinner: you never know what's going to arrive. The potluck table juxtaposes Swedish meatballs and hot ham buns and chicken empanadas and basil fried rice and, somehow, it all *works*. The uncanny diversity is half the fun. You never knew that watermelon and chorizo went together until they were set beside each other on the potluck table.

The unplanned variety of the potluck also *works* because the people who sign up for a potluck are people willing to be surprised. Each of these dishes on the table comes with a story. Behind each is a person with a history, a constellation of gifts and passions, a swirl of hurts and hopes—every one of them a cosmos of infinite dignity and complexity. This is why Amar says that at the heart of "neighboring" is a *holy curiosity*. Being a neighbor begins in wonder. *I wonder what* that *is on the table? Who made it? Where did they learn to make it? Can they teach me how?* The table becomes a place of communion, a place to practice what Amar calls the discipline of "spiritual accompaniment." As a place to witness the stories of others, the table is a site of *with*-ness. Around the potluck table, we are bound together not by sameness but by the shared experience of our difference. Around such a table, difference is no longer experienced as a threat but as a gift.

—

When did we stop signing up for potlucks? How did we lose our sense of curiosity? What do we lose when we're no longer willing to be surprised?

It is a sad commentary on the state of civil society that Amar's proposal to be neighborly might sound either naive or radical—as if the "greatest commandment" isn't to love God and love our neighbors (Matt. 22:36–40). But maybe that *is* radical today. Skeptical or dismissive responses to such an endeavor highlight something important: neighboring is an act of resistance and hope. To be a neighbor is to resist those principalities and powers and ideologies that want us to see every other person as either "us" or "them." Being a neighbor, and seeing fellow citizens as neighbors, is subversive of polarizing ideologies that pursue power and profit at the expense of community. To learn to live as neighbors is an expression of hope that we can be human together. Indeed, Amar cites Bishop Desmond Tutu's Ubuntu principle, reminding us we can only be human *together*: "I am a person through other people." Or, as one of my favorite philosophers, G. W. F. Hegel, once put it, we will find freedom when we recognize the "'I' that is 'We' and the 'We' that is 'I.'"

I think this is why Amar emphasizes the practices of neighboring as essentially *local*. Ideological demonization plays out in the abstraction of national discourse and media. These abstractions and stereotypes founder when we actually meet fellow citizens around the intimacy of a table, or when we care for one another's children, or when we work alongside them for the shared good of neighborhood parks and local libraries. In these intimate, local encounters and collaborations we realize that while we have different histories and different traditions and even different faiths, we share important *desires* that make us human.

Neighboring is local because it has to be *incarnate*. This is a final aspect of Amar's project that I want to highlight. While he is inviting us to be neighbors across deep religious difference, he in no way wants us to diminish those differences or dilute our religious convictions to arrive at some mushy, bland lowest common denominator. At a potluck, you don't throw all the dishes into a blender! Amar encourages us to bring all of our religious differences with us and put them on the table. The commonality imagined is not the result of mere sameness or similarity but rather one forged from *with*-ness.

Amar models this for us. He puts his own Christian commitments on the table. But as he powerfully reminds us, to be a Jesus follower and Christ imitator is to worship a God who takes the risk of being vulnerable in the incarnation—by becoming enfleshed. In a beautiful passage, Amar puts it this way: "Why does our good God come to us enfleshed? Why does God humble Godself to the form of creation? Why does God dive into the waves of cause and effect set in motion by God's very breath? Why does God desire a body that can be broken and bruised and demands nourishment and rest? Why does God choose to break bread and heal the sick with calloused hands? The answer is simple and profoundly beautiful: *to give it all away*" (p. 34). As steeped as we are in capitalist logic, this sounds like madness. *To give it all away* means to lose. But the logic of love is a very different economy: in the giving, love only expands, deepens, swells. If this book can convince more Jesus followers to be Christ imitators by giving away their defensiveness and insularity, to risk even their security, we can dream of a swelling tide of love, burbling up from the local, that could flood an entire nation. Here's hoping.

James K. A. Smith

INTRODUCTION

> "There are no unsacred places;
> there are only sacred places
> and desecrated places."
>
> —Wendell Berry, "How to Be a Poet (to Remind Myself)"

> "So, it is love, after all, that humbles me—the only surface that reflects the invisible divine. The only medium that transmits the sound of the spirit."
>
> —John West
> *Lessons and Carols: A Meditation on Recovery*

Can you *imagine* a world where we become neighbors to one another? Amid our struggles and divisions, can you envision a shared, communal table where people are joined together across their differences? Can you close your eyes and picture who might be sitting to your left and right? Whose presence makes your heart skip a beat? What dishes do you smell? What languages do you hear? What will you contribute?

This book is about the pursuit of the common good through a faith formed by and toward love of neighbor. It has in mind what and who we will be to each other in this cultural moment and in the moments to come. At the heart of this work is a simple but critical question: *How will we live?*

Cultivating this shared vision of the common good is a deeply local task. The key to shared flourishing for our neighborhoods is not located beyond the stars—if only we could build ideological spaceships to capture it. Instead, communities thrive when we turn our gaze horizontally toward our neighbors and the world around us. Contained in every person is an endless galaxy of beliefs and experiences, of joys and sorrows, of fears and comforts.[1] Any meaningful pursuit of a common good will require us to know our neighbors.

What will draw Christians toward common action toward the common good, though, is not only shared belief; it is also shared

1. The German theologian Friedrich Schleiermacher famously locates the infinitude that religion pursues in the individual. *On Religion: Speeches to Its Cultured Despisers*, ed. Richard Crouter, 2nd ed. (Cambridge University Press, 1996).

desire. We must become a people whose faith and desire are nurtured, formed, and cultivated by love for our neighbors. When we join with others in this common life, we are drawn into the vast expanse of their infinity just as they are drawn into ours. This neighbor-loving work not only changes what we believe about our neighbors; it also transforms how we relate to them. They are no longer enemies to fight; they are people to love. They are no longer social media handles or digital avatars; they are complex humans who are motivated by their deep values and their felt vulnerabilities. If we seek the shared flourishing of our community, we must desire right relationship with our neighbors.

Seeking the common good through this local practice of neighbor love is messy and complicated work. It would be far easier to remain aloof and simply read about our "neighbors" in books and surveys or make assumptions about them based on their yard signs. However, cultivating a truly common good requires humble proximity where our beliefs and assumptions about one another are challenged by the lived experiences of our neighbors. Our shared flourishing is impossible unless we enter into a common life where we are formed by and toward one another. Throughout this book, I use a simple illustration to describe this space: the table.

The table where the common good is cultivated recognizes and honors the goodness of all who are seated around it. At the table, people of different faiths, cultures, traditions, and beliefs are valued as partners in the work of loving and joining. Shared flourishing is not a zero-sum game, and we are not competitors. As neighbors, we come bearing our community's best "dishes," eager to share our wisdom, liturgies, and practices with others. It is marked by a desire for conversation, not conversion, for shared action, not stubborn arguments.

The table also reminds us that goodness is not hidden behind a locked church door. Our God is too generous to reserve goodness for any one people or keep it stored in one place. Our pursuit of the common good must recognize and honor the goodness present in those outside our tradition. We must acknowledge that this work of cultivating a common good has long been happening outside the church. At the table, we cannot eat only what we brought. Our plates must be filled with our neighbors' dishes as well.

It is true that Christians have often failed to do this well. Our relationship to the table has historically been marked by either absence or domination. We either refuse to join in this neighborly work or, if we do show up, we walk past our seats, grab the microphone, and assume we are running the meeting. That said, the task of this book is not to diagnose or examine all the ways that we have fallen short of joining in this shared work of communal flourishing. Instead, I offer a humble plea: *take a seat*. Join God's good and redemptive work already present here.

I am convinced that the more we attend to the needs of our community, the more attuned we will be to God's good purposes and actions in the world. The more we can open ourselves to the possibility of love—even love across our deep disagreements—the more we will find ourselves looking and living like Christ in our world. This isn't a transactional love; it is a selfless love. This is a pursuit of a common good formed in and by a neighborly faith that sees the world as braided together in a dance of mutual flourishing and radical love.[2] This is a commitment to nurturing our community, which includes both the places we inhabit and the people we dwell in them with.

The common good is not found; it is built in community. Seeking the common good begins by walking across the street, knocking on our neighbor's door, and entering into relationship with them. This means we must open ourselves to the possibility of love—both bestowing love upon others and receiving love for ourselves. We must look around us and witness the rituals, stories, beliefs, and traditions our communities instill deep meaning into. We must rec-

2. Norman Wirzba, *Love's Braided Dance: Hope in a Time of Crisis* (Yale University Press, 2024).

ognize that any meaningful vision of the common good will bind together our flourishing with the flourishing of our neighbors. As the poet Christian Wiman concludes, "The revelation we want—or at any rate the revelation we need—is not ultimate, but intimate."[3] A meaningful vision of the common good grows in the intimate relationship of neighbors living and loving together.

—

Writing at the height of the COVID-19 pandemic, singer-songwriter Jensen McRae released a song titled "Immune." Amid the deep divides across America stressed by the ever-present reality of sickness and death, she asks a simple question: "What will we be to each other if the world doesn't end?"[4]

We again live—or perhaps never cease to live—in a moment that feels as if humanity's future hangs in the balance. The trouble with these moments is that, if the world is going to end, we can find our way to justify almost anything. When we believe our entire future depends on the outcome of a presidential election, vaccine mandate, position of leadership, or government policy, we will go to great lengths to ensure that we are on the "winning" side.

But what will we be to each other if the world doesn't end? What will we say to each other when, after doing all we can to secure our power and desires, the world continues to spin and we must live with one another? What will we be to each other when, after speaking the most hateful and vile rhetoric about those who are different from us, we must share a community? What will we do when we encounter the reality of our neighbors at the community center or grocery store? How will we live with those we call our enemies as we share a hospital, playground, softball league, or congregation?

3. Christian Wiman, *Zero at the Bone: Fifty Entries Against Despair* (New York: Farrar, Straus & Giroux, 2023), 227.

4. Jensen McRae, "Immune," written by Rahki and Jensen McRae (Human Re Sources, 2021).

The philosopher Søren Kierkegaard explains that it is hard to distinguish followers of Christ from those who only admire him until the cost of following him is counted—until we must decide what and who we will be to one another when love, kindness, justice, and a common good come at a heavy price.[5] What defines a follower of Christ today is the willingness—the *desire*—to follow God into the neighborhood and join God at the table. In a world marked by violence, opposition, division, and hatred, God is calling us to meet our neighbors in the thin spaces of goodness and love amid a world that is not as it should be. Where admirers of Christ observe from afar, followers of Christ will take up this call to love, seek goodness, and join in communities of belonging.

This is where the common good begins: with the inclination to love even when it doesn't make sense, to share even when we lack, to listen even when we disagree, to dream even when we despair, and to seek the good of our neighbor even when they might not do the same for us. Any truly common good lifts up the well-being of the public—the commons—across our many differences.

The question bears repeating: *How will we live?* Amid our differences and disagreements, through the strife and terror of our world, through the reality of death and the hope of resurrection, the answer for Christians is clear. We live as neighbors.

5. Whereas an admirer keeps themselves personally detached from the object of their admiration, "a follower is or strives to be what he admires." Søren Kierkegaard, *Provocations: Spiritual Writings of Kierkegaard*, comp. and ed. Charles E. Moore (Orbis Books, 2003), 86.

1

COMING TO THE TABLE

"And in this thinking together we begin to see what we had not seen before: we belong to each other, we belong together. Belonging must become the hermeneutic starting point from which we think the social, the political, the individual, the ecclesial, and most crucial for this work, the educational."

—Willie James Jennings
After Whiteness: An Education in Belonging

"It comes to this: of whatever sort it is,
it must be 'lit with piercing glances into the life of things';
it must acknowledge the spiritual forces which have made it."

—Marianne Moore, "When I Buy Pictures"

We arrived at Tabernacle Community Baptist Church on a bright April evening. Pulling into a parking spot across the street, I heard an enthusiastic volunteer shout, "Are you here for the Common Ground meeting? Come on in. The food is hot!" Mark and I followed the volunteer through the side entrance of the church and made our way to a basement overflowing with the warm and welcoming smell of a potluck. Gathered to greet us were hundreds of organizers, small-business owners, beat reporters, local officials, religious leaders, and more, all seated at long rows of tables to talk about equitable housing practices, affordable health care, police reform, and public education.

Two decades ago, Mark served as the first lead organizer for Common Ground, a collection of congregations, organizations, coalitions, and neighborhood groups in Milwaukee, Wisconsin. We sat at a table near the back to hear about all that Common Ground, now forty thousand members strong, was doing in and for our city. For two hours, community leaders stepped up to the microphone to share stories of hope, raise issues that needed support, and provide updates on legacy projects. The roll call included retired teachers leading a "Get out the Vote" campaign, young organizers protesting unjust living conditions for tenants at a nearby apartment complex, and the leaders of a local parish organizing a service day in the Riverwest neighborhood. Across their many differences, what brought these leaders to a common table was a shared desire to see our city and all its residents flourish.

Cultivating a shared vision of the common good begins in the neighborhood. It starts in the church basement where community organizers meet and the town hall where residents advocate for stop signs on busy streets. It takes root at the neighborhood potluck where everyone brings a dish to pass, the coffee shop where students gather to share big ideas, and the library where knowledge and resources are made accessible to the community.

The common good is created at a shared table where each person brings the best of their community's beliefs, experiences, religions, cultures, and languages and offers it to the whole. The chairs around this table are filled with pastors and imams, small-business owners and local officials, teachers and artists, organizers and nonprofit leaders. Seated together, we begin to envision a loving way of being with and for one another as we seek the shared flourishing of our entire community.

Joining in this work is a daunting task. Opening ourselves to the possibility of becoming neighbors amid deep difference and disagreement is not for the faint of heart. Waiting for us are difficult conversations about how communities have harmed one another, challenges to our blind spots, and lingering questions of whether this loving work is truly possible. Seeking the common good is messy and unpredictable because communities, like the people they contain, are complicated. However, in my experience, the most meaningful visions of shared flourishing and the common good are created through this intimate, joining work where we link our arms together and commit to love and serve our neighbors.[1] Without this, the common good is reduced to whatever is good for the greatest number of people. But when we come together in this loving way,

1. Intimacy and eroticism, Willie Jennings explains, "have been so commodified and sexualized that we Christians have turned away from them in fear that they irredeemably signify sexual antinomianism, moral chaos, and sin, or at least the need to police such words and the power they invoke. But intimacy and eroticism speak of our birthright formed in the body of Jesus and the protocols of breaking, sharing, touching, tasting, and seeing the goodness of God." *After Whiteness: An Education in Belonging* (Eerdmans, 2020), 11.

we create a vision of the common good that includes the whole of the community, not just one part.

The presence of deep difference raises an important question for us: How can our communities thrive if our most fundamental, core beliefs about morality, virtue, and goodness are drawn from different wells? One answer is that our traditions and the values within them benefit the whole when they are placed in service to the greater community.[2] Our neighborhoods thrive when faith communities arrive at a shared table to freely offer the stories, beliefs, and wisdom literature that inform how they show up in the world. This doesn't mean we compromise our beliefs or water them down. Instead, we recognize that the goal of the table is not conversion or debate; it is shared flourishing and the good of the whole. In a world that assumes that deep difference and spiteful division cannot be separated, the table demonstrates how our differences are not obstacles to overcome; they are gifts to this common life.

The Table

The table is a tangible and salient image of the common good. Think of it this way: we spend most of our lives around tables. We gather around them to eat. We sit at them with a warm cup of chai. We stack books on them at the local library. They hold our picnic baskets at the local park and our exams in the classroom. They're attached to the back of every seat on an airplane and create community spaces on train cars. Tables, like the possibility of a common good, are all around us. They exist in ordinary spaces where people gather, converse, read, eat, and worship.

The table represents the practice of intentional hospitality—of

2. See Jeffrey Stout, *Democracy and Tradition* (Princeton University Press, 2005). Also Hartmut Rosa, *Democracy Needs Religion*, trans. Valentine A. Pakis (Polity, 2024).

making room when we are under no obligation to do so.[3] When we center our communities around the table, we consider how much food is available, how many chairs can fit comfortably, what each person is bringing, and how to make space when someone knocks at the door asking if there is room for a few more. A table offers us a sacred place of belonging with an invitation to join. When neighbors are brought together in this way, we can completely and radically reimagine what our common life looks like.

What I find powerful about the table is that it centers our humanity through the shared experience of hunger. The table provides us with a simple task: take and eat. When we sit at the table, we lead with empty stomachs eager to be filled. As our bodies are physically nourished by the food spread across the table, our souls are spiritually nourished as the stories contained in the meal are shared. In this shared proximity, we are reminded that our flourishing is interdependent. We are made to be together—to look one another in the eye and feel our shared humanity.[4]

—

The table has long been tied to the Christian practice of neighboring.[5] Throughout the Gospels, Jesus is often found at or around the table. He eats with Mary and Martha, infusing their table interaction with spiritual weight (Luke 10:38–42). Jesus's first miracle—turning water to wine—happens at a wedding feast in Cana, a venue

3. Christine D. Pohl, *Making Room: Recovering Hospitality as a Christian Tradition*, twenty-fifth anniversary ed. (Eerdmans, 2024).

4. Norman Wirzba rightly explains that, "From an ecological and theological standpoint . . . flourishing requires the well-being of bodies together." *Food and Faith: A Theology of Eating*, 2nd ed. (Cambridge University Press, 2019), 175.

5. See Robert J. Karris, *Eating Your Way Through Luke's Gospel* (Liturgical Press, 2006); Matthew Croasmun and Miroslav Volf, *The Hunger for Home: Food and Meals in the Gospel of Luke* (Baylor University Press, 2022); Craig L. Blomberg, *Contagious Holiness: Jesus' Meals with Sinners*, New Studies in Biblical Theology (InterVarsity Press, 2005).

filled with tables of joyful fellowship (John 2:1–11). He miraculously feeds five thousand who gathered to hear him speak and perform miracles, turning a shoreline into a gigantic table of providence (Matt. 14:13–21).

Jesus also uses the table to subvert the social order of his day by dining with those who were considered outcasts or impure. At a dinner with religious leaders, Jesus is anointed by a woman with an alabaster jar of precious ointment (Luke 7:36–38). He calls Zacchaeus, the chief tax collector, down from a tree and invites him to the table (Luke 19:1–10). At a gathering with religious leaders, Jesus teaches that they ought to invite "the poor, the crippled, the lame, and the blind," rather than the rich and notable members of their community (Luke 14:12–14).[6] Around the table, Jesus proclaims that tax collectors and sex workers will enter the kingdom ahead of the religious elite of his time (Matt. 21:31–32; Mark 2:15; Luke 11:37–54).

In his gospel, John places the table at the heart of Christian community. During the Last Supper, Jesus teaches his disciples that "he had come from God and was going to God" (13:3) by bending down to wash their feet while they reclined at the table. After modeling this path of service, humility, and sacrifice, Jesus then offers his final instructions and fuses his teaching into a practice of blessing, breaking, and giving of bread and wine.[7] It is fitting that this table practice defines God's people: *communion*.

Of course, Jesus's table fellowship does not end at the Last Supper. In his resurrected body, Jesus walks with two disciples on the

6. All scripture quotations are from the New Revised Standard Version Updated Edition (NRSVUE) unless otherwise indicated. New Revised Standard Version, Updated Edition. 2021 National Council of Churches of Christ in the United States of America.

7. The theme of blessing, breaking, and giving is expounded and elaborated upon in several books by Eugene Peterson, including *Christ Plays in Ten Thousand Places: A Conversation in Spiritual Theology* (Eerdmans, 2008), and *The Jesus Way: A Conversation on the Ways That Jesus Is the Way* (Eerdmans, 2011).

road to Emmaus. It is in the middle of dining and breaking bread with them that the two strangers see that they are in the presence of Jesus (Luke 24:13–35). Jesus also appears to his disciples on the Sea of Tiberias, again turning the shoreline into a table of connection and fellowship (John 21:4–14; Luke 24:36–43). Soon after, Jesus eats breakfast with Peter and asks him three times if Peter loves him. In doing so, Jesus covers Peter's thrice denial with both the nourishment of food and the covenant of grace (John 21:15–19). When describing his future ascension, Jesus explains that he must go and prepare a place for his followers (John 14:3), a place described as a great banquet table (Isa. 25:6; 55:1–2; Matt. 8:11–12).

If we are looking for Christ in the world today, we will likely find him at the table.

—

It does not take long, though, to see that the church has failed to live up to this vision of the table. The pattern of Christians wielding their power to promote their gain over and against the good of those outside their community is well-known, and its consequences are nothing short of tragic. While it is right to reckon with these large-scale evils and patterns of domination, working against the common good in our communities today often doesn't look like crusades, chattel slavery, or colonial expansion. It looks like Christians who practice rigid exclusion by building spiritual—and sometimes physical—walls around their tables and placing guards at the gate. It also looks like reckless inclusion, where Christians open the doors to their table but fail to practice true hospitality by considering what it means to have a diverse collection of people gathered together.[8]

On the ground, we see this lived out in the everyday actions

8. Matthew Kaemingk uses a threefold illustration of a "wall," "door," and "table" in his insightful book *Christian Hospitality and Muslim Immigration in an Age of Fear* (Eerdmans, 2018), 268–99.

of Christians in our community who abuse, manipulate, ignore, gaslight, and slander their neighbors. It is the pastor who teaches vaguely of God's love and our obedience without ever engaging with the messy, unloving parts of the Bible.[9] It is the Christian food pantry volunteer who manipulates those in need to say the sinner's prayer to gain access to groceries and supplies. It is the politician who claims the banner of Christianity while dismissing Christ's command to love our neighbors, show mercy, and turn the other cheek.[10]

We also work against the common good when we fail to reckon with the lived experiences of our neighbors in and beyond the pews. This looks like preachers who emphatically pound their pulpits with the American flag on their right side, preaching a message of "God, guns, and glory" while students don't feel safe in the classroom; like calls to repentance that end with tepid platitudes like "be kind to your coworker" while protestors march in the streets outside to decry systems of injustice and exploitation; like Christmas sermons that celebrate Christ as a refugee king but fail to acknowledge the hu-

9. Think here of Paul's instruction for slaves to obey their master; the pentateuchal laws about food and determinations of impurity that overtly subject women to rituals of cleanliness; God's condoning of mass violence against unbelieving communities; and the prophets' likening of Israel to an unfaithful spouse deserving of wrath. See Jill Hicks-Keeton, *Good Book: How White Evangelicals Save the Bible to Save Themselves* (Fortress, 2023).

10. In an NPR interview with Scott Detrow, evangelical leader Russell Moore explains that pastors preaching the Sermon on the Mount are met with congregants asking, "Where did you get those liberal talking points?" Moore explains, "What was alarming to me is that in most of these scenarios, when the pastor would say, 'I'm literally quoting Jesus Christ' the response would not be, 'I apologize.' The response would be, 'Yes, but that doesn't work anymore. That's weak.' And when we get to the point where the teachings of Jesus himself are seen as subversive to us, then we're in a crisis." Scott Detrow, Gabriel J. Sánchez, and Sarah Handel, "He Was a Top Church Official Who Criticized Trump. He Says Christianity Is in Crisis," NPR, August 8, 2023, https://tinyurl.com/4kjm6e5v.

manity of refugees and asylum seekers at the southern border; like Bible studies that encourage attendees to serve the "least of these" while ICE (Immigration and Customs Enforcement) officers disappear undocumented immigrants in their congregation; and like pastors who praise an indescribable, uncontainable, unfathomable, way-maker God but cannot fathom what it might look like to create space for queer people in their sanctuary.

How, then, do we come to the table? How do we show up in this space with humility and curiosity? The solution to these patterns and practices that drive Christians away from the table is not topical; it is transfusive. To meaningfully come to the table, we cannot begrudgingly sit in the farthest seat with our hands cupped over our ears. We must become people who *desire* the table. We must be willing to be formed by and toward life together with our neighbors. As Pope Francis explains, "It is one thing to feel forced to live together, but something entirely different to value the richness and beauty of those seeds of common life that need to be sought out and cultivated."[11]

To rightly come to the table, we must be compelled by and drawn to spaces where difference and diversity are treated as gifts. In a social and political climate that gives us free license to be cruel and hateful, we must become a people who truly give a damn about our neighbors and their well-being. We must look at the kind of people we are and are becoming. To do this, we must cultivate a faith that is formed by and toward love for our neighbors.

Desiring the Table

Faith is often spoken of as an object or attribute that we possess. Christians are people "of faith" who "have faith" in Jesus Christ. Faith is something we can cling to or abandon—that we either have

11. Francis, *Fratelli Tutti*, October 3, 2020, https://tinyurl.com/k2wrp5hd. I am grateful to Dr. Ki Joo Choi for directing me to this beautiful letter.

or lose. We pick up faith as we stroll through life's long road. This makes faith quantifiable: one person can have "more faith" than another. Jesus seems to point to this when he rebukes his disciples before calming the storm and sea, "Why are you afraid, you of little faith?" (Matt. 8:26); and when he instructs them that faith "the size of a mustard seed" can move a mountain (Matt. 17:20).

In practice, though, faith is not so straightforward and static. Like desire, faith is dynamic, evolving, and ever-moving. Faith does not "grow" like a savings account; rather, faith increases like a child who matures into an adult or a flower that blossoms in the spring. If Jesus's mustard seed illustration teaches us anything, it is that the quantity of faith matters little. What is of greatest importance is the substance, posture, form, and direction of faith. Faith, explains eco-theologian Norman Wirzba, is "a loving way of being that is animated by an affirmation of the goodness of this life." It is "a practiced way of life rooted in the conviction that this life is worth cherishing, defending, and celebrating."[12] Faith is formed.

This formation happens as faith responds to God's loving action in the world at the site of finite impossibility and divine possibility.[13] Faith is formed as it moves toward God in pursuit of those sacred, fleeting moments where we feel as though we've been mysteriously grasped by something outside of us—when the transcendent breaks

12. Norman Wirzba is talking here about hope, but these words can also be applied to faith. *Love's Braided Dance: Hope in a Time of Crisis* (Yale University Press, 2024), 16–17.

13. Kierkegaard explains it this way: "The decisive thing is: for God everything is possible. This is eternally true and therefore true every moment. People no doubt say this in the ordinary way of things, and this is how one ordinarily puts it, but the decisive moment only comes when man is brought to the utmost extremity, where in human terms there is no possibility. Then the question is whether he will believe that for God everything is possible, that is, whether he will have faith." Søren Kierkegaard, *Sickness unto Death: A Christian Psychological Exposition for Upbuilding and Awakening*, trans. and ed. Howard V. Hong and Edna H. Hong (Princeton University Press, 1980).

into our atmosphere and calls out to us. As the French-born Indian monk Abhishiktananda poetically describes, "Faith . . . is to recognize and accept that we are face to face with our God, to realize the presence of that fundamental love which makes us to be, and opens up in God immeasurable abysses of grace and mercy."[14]

Faith is the polyphonic hum of belief and devotion. It begins with the glimmering incantation of our souls. *O God, you are my God. . . . My soul clings to you* (Ps. 63:1, 8). It blooms when our endless hunger and longings meet the divine reality that God is with us here and now.[15] Faith is the gentle vibration of the Spirit that lives in us, providing the baseline of hope. It is our orientation to God and the world. Even if all else is stripped away, the hum remains. *Christ with me, Christ before me, Christ behind me, Christ in me.*

—

This formation of faith through devotion to God directly transforms our desires. Saint Augustine describes this process as the ability to discern what God has given us to use (*uti*) and to enjoy (*frui*).[16] To *enjoy* something is to love something—like God and our neighbors—for its own sake. To *use* something is to care about that thing because it brings us closer to what we *enjoy*. For example, we desire the common table because it provides a shared space for us to love our neighbors. The table is used toward the pursuit of a greater enjoyment of God and others.

What keeps Christians from the table is that we get this wrong: we enjoy the things we should use, and we use the things we should enjoy. Augustine illustrates this by describing a community residing in a foreign land whose only desire is to return home. As they

14. Abhishiktananda, *Prayer*, new ed. (Canterbury Press, 2006), 16.

15. Karl Barth argues that God's continual breaking-in to creation should fundamentally shape how we perceive and engage in the world. *God Here and Now*, trans. Paul M. van Buren (Routledge, 2003).

16. Oliver O'Donovan, "'Usus' and 'Fruitio' in Augustine, 'De Doctrina Christiana I,'" *Journal of Theological Studies*, n.s., 33, pt. 2 (October 1982): 361–97.

embark on this journey, though, they become so infatuated with the horses, carriages, and ships transporting them that they forget about the very place to which they are going. Augustine's point isn't that horses and ships are not worthy of our attention, but rather that the travelers loved them so much that they forgot their true and ultimate love: their homeland. The travelers mistook what was only meant to be used as something to enjoy.[17]

The same is true today when Christians enjoy the table as our highest pursuit but then neglect to care for the people present at it. We begin to love the table so much that we never get up from it and move out into the world to serve others. We also see this disordered desire among Christians who treat power, control, influence, and prestige as something to *enjoy* rather than to *use* for the greater good of our community. These are a clear sign that our desires are malformed.[18]

What will bring us to the table of shared, communal flourishing is a desire to *enjoy* both God and neighbor in and for themselves. In other words, our love of God directs and catalyzes our love of neighbor, just as the enjoyment of our neighbor orients and energizes our love for God. We do not love our neighbors to get something greater from them or from God. We love our neighbors because they, made in the image of God, are worthy of love. We seek their good and well-being because they are our neighbors. We care about the quality and depth of these relationships because Jesus tells us this is the path to relationships of mutual flourishing. We come to the table because the people we love are there too.

—

Rightly ordering our loves, though, is not as simple as believing or saying the right things. We must pay attention to how faith and our

17. Kevin W. Hector offers a more robust treatment of this illustration in *Christianity as a Way of Life: A Systematic Theology* (Yale University Press, 2023), 33.

18. I offer an extended commentary on this in my essay "Can Christians End Our Quest for Control?" *Sojourners*, June 2025, https://tinyurl.com/5h6pufjt.

lived experience work together. We do not only hold ideas about Christianity in our minds. Faith lives in our souls and our bodies. To cultivate the wisdom and discernment of use and enjoyment, we must recognize the formative influence that lies within the places and communities we inhabit.[19]

In his book *Desiring the Kingdom*, James K. A. Smith offers a helpful illustration: the local shopping mall, which Smith memorably calls the "cathedral of consumerism." In this cathedral, we are not aimless wanderers, even when we go only to pass the time. No, the mall has its own rites and rituals of spending, buying, eating, and watching. It also holds a central message preached through advertisements and announcements: "This will make you happy!" The mall is intentionally designed to shape our desires.[20]

The church is another example of a building whose purpose is revealed in its design. From the stained-glass windows to the historic liturgies of sacrament and gospel proclamation to the coffee station in the church lobby, the local congregation is an intentionally formative space created to engage our mind, soul, and body.[21] Some churches have even sought to name this explicitly by exchanging the language of "service" for "experience." When we raise our hands in worship, recite the creeds in community, bow our heads in prayer, kneel in a posture of confession, and partake in the bread and wine of the Lord's table, faith is infused with our experience of God and the world. This infusion changes us and our desires.

Of course, it is not only physical spaces that form us but also the people we share those spaces with. In his work against South African apartheid, Bishop Desmond Tutu often invoked the Zulu

19. James K. A. Smith, *How to Inhabit Time: Understanding the Past, Facing the Future, Living Faithfully Now* (Baker Books, 2022). See also Smith, *You Are What You Love: The Spiritual Power of Habit* (Brazos, 2016).

20. James K. A. Smith, *Desiring the Kingdom: Worship, Worldview, and Cultural Formation* (Brazos, 2009), 19–23.

21. See Hanna Reichel's work on conceptual design in *After Method: Queer Grace, Conceptual Design, and the Possibility of Theology* (Westminster John Knox, 2023).

concept of Ubuntu, which communicates, "I am a person through other people. My humanity is tied to yours." In other words, Ubuntu reminds us of what it means to be human. Bishop Tutu and leaders like him argued that true freedom and peace cannot be achieved as long as people remain in chains.[22] We are *who* we are because of the people around us.

The table where the common good is cultivated forms us spatially and relationally. Our presence at the table not only forms others; it also forms us by shifting our imagination of the world and our place in it. When we are formed by the table, we are drawn toward what Wirzba describes as "the life force and the creative energy that propel people to risk giving themselves to others."[23] This is the work of joining—yes, in love and compassion, but also in pain and plight. Our shared desire for the table invites us into a greater desire for a loving, proximate relationship with one another. It is in these places and relationships that our desires are shaped toward the table where we gather. At the table, we participate in a common life.

Joining at the Table

After Jesus's ascension into heaven, his followers return to the table in an anxious waiting for what might happen next. What will become of this unlikely community that has joined together on the Way? How will they live together in the absence of Christ's dwelling among them?

The answer arrives in a miraculous way. At Pentecost, the Holy Spirit descends on those gathered in Jerusalem like a flame caught up in a violent wind and fills the home where the first followers of

22. See Desmond Mpilo Tutu, *No Future Without Forgiveness* (Doubleday, 1999); also Nelson Mandela, *Long Walk to Freedom: The Autobiography of Nelson Mandela* (Little, Brown, 1994), and Michael Battle, *Desmond Tutu: A Spiritual Biography of South Africa's Confessor* (Westminster John Knox, 2021).

23. Wirzba, *Love's Braided Dance*, 20.

Jesus are gathered. The Holy Spirit, though, does not come with a single, unifying tongue that those gathered could all understand. Instead, she comes in "divided tongues, as of fire," giving those present the ability to speak in other tongues (Acts 2:3–4). The first act of the Holy Spirit at Pentecost is the mysterious and paradoxical work of joining.

Pentecost is a simultaneously fantastic and intimate moment. Indeed, to hear one's native tongue in an unexpected or unfamiliar place is often an emotional experience. In a chaotic and sudden moment, the foreigner and refugee hear God speak in their native language. In a new land, they recognize the percussive tones and familiar timbre spoken by their loved ones—their auntie and *abuelita*. By coming in a multitude of languages, the Spirit beckons those gathered to unite as followers of Jesus by embracing and asking one another, "What did God say to you?"[24] To understand God's revelation, these followers must participate in loving community across their many differences. Yes, this is where the work of joining begins for the Christian church. Pentecost is not what these spirit-longing people asked for or expected, but it is the gift God has for them. It is the disruptive, baffling, and holy work of forming a new community.[25]

Following Jesus's example of radical table fellowship, the shared table became a source of spiritual and physical nourishment for the early church (Acts 2:46). It is through the mediation of a shared table that Jews and gentiles learned to live together under the lordship of Christ (Acts 10:9–16; 11:1–18). The New Testament letters written by the leaders of the early church also contain instruction about enjoying and sharing in this fellowship (1 Cor. 10:15–17), calling the

24. I first heard this imagined scenario told by Dr. Eric D. Barreto in a Princeton Seminary course titled "Race and Ethnicity in the New Testament."

25. Some aspects of this telling are adapted from an essay I wrote about Pentecost in *Sojourners*. See Amar D. Peterman, "There's No Such Thing as Colorblind Christianity," *Sojourners*, August 18, 2021, https://tinyurl.com/4t8afzem. See also Keri Day, *Notes of a Native Daughter: Testifying in Theological Education* (Eerdmans, 2021).

church to practice hospitality (Heb. 13:2; 1 Pet. 4:9) and show no partiality (James 2:1–13). In the book of Revelation, John describes a divine vision of an eternal meal: the marriage supper of the Lamb (Rev. 9:6–10).

This joining work, though, is not easy. As the memory of Pentecost begins to fade, the struggles of finding a common good amid a multitude of differences become evident. Fraught with all the complexities that accompany humans attempting to live together, in ordinary time, the early church navigated and negotiated within a world divinely called to unity in difference. Philip must love and baptize an Ethiopian eunuch (Acts 8); Peter must break bread with a Roman named Cornelius (Acts 10); Jews and gentiles must share a community (Acts 15); Paul must find God in the altars of Athens (Acts 17); and believers like Timothy who live between Jewish and gentile heritage must question if this ethnic straddling is an obstacle to gospel proclamation (Acts 16).

Gathered under the lordship of Christ, zealots and tax collectors, enslaved and free, rich and poor, eunuchs and sex workers, beggars and bankers, fishermen and scholars, magicians and stargazers all learned to dwell together, share food and drink, carry one another's burdens, love deeply, and join together in radical, table intimacy.[26]

—

The faith demonstrated by the early church is markedly a faith *in* Christ *for* others. It is a faith that emphasizes a positive intervention in the lives of those we love. It is a faith that moves mountains and hearts. It is a faith that overcomes the systems and structures designed to exclude so that we might create communities that flourish together. It is a faith that reimagines communities and redesigns the spaces we inhabit to form us toward love and hope.

26. Willie James Jennings, *Acts: A Theological Commentary on the Bible* (Westminster John Knox, 2017).

Faith and desire, when rightly formed by the light of Christ, have the immense and incredible power to bring about a common good for our communities. Directed by and toward love, the gaze of our imagination, dreams, and creative energies will also shift from our individual comfort to the needs of our neighbors. To imagine in this way is to create and dream of new ways of being in and relating to the world. This godly imagination of wholeness helps us recognize the beauty of our traditions and the good desire to place our experience alongside those around us. This recognition stirs in us the holy desire to become more loving, empathic, just, and hospitable people.

When our faith is formed toward love, how we imagine the world begins to change. This creative work of imagination at the table is a compelling and beautiful witness to the gospel of Christ today that does not prescribe a set of beliefs but instead invites others to participate in a story still being told. We gather at the table to tell a story of flourishing and goodness that is still being written. I believe this is what God is calling us to.

2

JOINING GOD IN THE NEIGHBORHOOD

"I'll be all aroun' in the dark. I'll be everywhere—wherever you look. Wherever they's a fight so hungry people can eat, I'll be there. Wherever they's a cop beatin' up a guy, I'll be there. If Casy knowed, why, I'll be in the way guys yell when they're mad an'—I'll be in the way kids laugh when they're hungry an' they know supper's ready. An' when our folks eat the stuff they raise an' live in the houses they build—why, I'll be there. See?"

—Tom Joad, in John Steinbeck, *The Grapes of Wrath*

"Beloved, let us love one another, because love is from God; everyone who loves is born of God and knows God. Whoever does not love does not know God, for God is love. God's love was revealed among us in this way: God sent his only Son into the world so that we might live through him. In this is love, not that we loved God but that he loved us and sent his Son to be the atoning sacrifice for our sins. Beloved, since God loved us so much, we also ought to love one another."

—1 John 4:7–11

I remember the first time I felt God calling me to the table. I was living in downtown Chicago when a small organization called Neighborly Faith offered me a scholarship to attend a conference hosted by the Interfaith Youth Core.[1] As an Indian American, I am familiar with sitting around tables with peers and elders of different faith traditions. However, I had never attended—let alone felt *called to*—an "interfaith" table where our differences would be laid out and placed alongside one another. I didn't know if this was a place for discussion or debate. I wondered if I could show up in the fullness of my Christian convictions about God and the world like I did with my South Asian friends, or if I would be instructed to leave them at the door.

On a warm August morning, I commuted into the city and arrived at the hotel on the Chicago riverwalk where the conference was held. I found a fellow classmate and we made our way to the registration desk, where a Muslim woman wearing a hijab warmly greeted us with a "Salaam Alaykum." After receiving a name badge and directory, we entered the main ballroom. It was filled with hundreds of students seated around tables, eating a colorful spread of food. Between bites, they were already eagerly engaged in conversation as

1. Interfaith Youth Core, now called Interfaith America, is a leading civic nonprofit that inspires, equips, and connects America's religious leaders and institutions to unlock the potential of America's religious diversity as we work together toward the common good.

we waited for the organization's founder and president, Eboo Patel, to make his opening remarks.

As I scanned the room for an open seat, I noticed that attendees weren't debating one another or shaking clenched fists. They were smiling, nodding, and listening intently. When I joined a table and introduced myself, I was wrapped up in this eager and mutual curiosity about how we all arrived at this place. When the time quickly came for the opening presentation, Eboo affirmed our curiosity with a short but memorable message: America is a potluck nation; and its promises of freedom, equality, and the pursuit of happiness are deeply intertwined with how each of us engages with people of different faiths.[2]

Throughout the weekend, I sat at table after table that explored and affirmed a commitment to one another's good. Together, we found that our differences were significant, but they were not an obstacle to friendship or shared action toward a common good. In fact, when our differences were placed under the shared goal of understanding and seeking one another's good, each of our respective traditions had something good and empowering to say about the other.

This conference—this calling to the table—was one of the most formative events in my life.[3] It offered a taste of how we might live together as a community and as a nation. It also gave me tangible steps and practices to make this vision a reality in my neighborhood.

2. Many of Eboo's remarks are contained in his book *Out of Many Faiths: Religious Diversity and the American Promise* (Princeton University Press, 2018), which was released shortly after this conference.

3. At this conference, I joined Interfaith America's Emerging Leaders Network, which provided resources, grants, and opportunities for me to continue participating in interfaith dialogue through college and seminary. The passion planted through Interfaith America has taken me to places I never could have imagined. After graduating from seminary, I joined the staff at Interfaith America, where I led this incredible network as assistant director of Civic Networks.

Perhaps most importantly, though, it gave me a national network of emerging leaders to pursue this work with. From this community of organizers, field builders, and bridge builders, one often-repeated question has fundamentally shaped how I understand our pursuit of the common good: *Where are all the Christians?*

—

Christians often veer far from the table because they fear gathering in this way might require them to compromise their beliefs. What if the table is actually a giant melting pot where all our distinct beliefs and ideas are thrown in and boiled down to a homogeneous muck? This is a worthy concern. In my experience, though, I have found the opposite is actually true: When we come to the table, we don't leave God at the door; we join God at the table. The "dishes" of our different traditions aren't melted together; they are honored, appreciated, and eaten alongside one another. Any table that requires us to throw our beliefs into the melting pot is not seeking a truly common good.

God's presence at the table beckons us to enter into vulnerable proximity with those in our community, just as Jesus did. God's good desire is for us to love one another in table fellowship. God is asking us to open ourselves to the possibility of radical and genuine love across our differences. Truly, if the call on every Christian's life is Christlikeness, then joining God at the common table is not optional.

Participating in God's good work means taking up practices that orient us to God and transform how we show up in the world.[4] These liturgies serve the ultimate task of the Christian: to live a life attuned to the Spirit's redeeming work in the world: in the places where people gather and laugh together, where we deliberate and debate, where we ponder the deep things of God, where we labor and

4. See Kevin W. Hector, *Christianity as a Way of Life: A Systematic Theology* (Yale University Press, 2023).

learn, and where we entertain and experience joy. The task before us is to bring our distinct, well-seasoned dishes of love, goodness, and community to offer to the potluck spread. We must join God where God is already at work: in the neighborhood.

A Call to Love

The first "dish" Christians can offer to the pursuit of a common good is a belief that God is love and that our highest calling is to love God and our neighbors. Love is worthy of our highest attention because *how* we love forms how we value, order, and prioritize all other things in our lives.[5] In other words, who, what, how, and why we love is the measuring rod for the kind of people we are and how we act in the world. Love shapes our actions, our values, and our concerns. It is the good that makes all other goods *good.*

This is why Jesus's command to love God and neighbor is so important. Any good and true love that Christians can offer to another must begin with the recognition that God first loved us. When the reality of this truth permeates our soul, we begin to model our love for others after the pattern of God's love for us, which is marked by radical self-giving, hospitality, justice, and grace. To will the good of the other is the purest form of neighbor love.[6]

Recognizing God's loving and caring action toward us, neighbor love requires us to love and care about others for their own sake—seeking their good and appreciating what is good about them.[7] As recipients of and respondents to God's love, we give of ourselves in loving others. To truly love our neighbors, then, is to enjoy them, to care

5. The philosopher Charles Taylor calls love a "hypergood" that directs all other goods. See *Sources of the Self: The Making of the Modern Identity* (Cambridge University Press, 1989).

6. Thomas Aquinas famously defines love as "to will the good of the other." See *Summa Theologiae* I-II, Q. 26, Art. 4.

7. Hector, *Christianity as a Way of Life*, 2.

about them for their own sake, and to seek their good precisely because they are our neighbors, loved by God and made in God's image.

When we fail to do this—to enjoy others *in God*—we are tempted by possessive loves that place the neighbor at the service of our own beliefs, goals, and interests.[8] But neighbor love is not utilitarian. We don't use our neighbors to get something from them. Instead, we love and enjoy our neighbors because God tells us to. This practice of giving, receiving, fostering, nurturing, and cultivating love wraps us up in the divine life of God as coheirs with Christ. The call to neighbor love is a call to participate in God's sustaining love for the world. To love God also means to love what God loves—other people, creation, and the communities we inhabit. It's about joining God's work in healing a wounded world, making love practical and embodied on earth as it is in heaven. In short, if we love God, we will seek to do God's will; and what God wills for us is to love one another just as God loves us.

Placing love for our neighbor within God's love for us also helps us veer far from the temptation to believe that seeking the good of those who do not seek our good is foolish. While I unequivocally believe that God is not calling us to self-harm of any kind, living into the command to love our friends, neighbors, and even our enemies bears witness to the breadth and length of God's redemptive love. Centering this self-giving love as the highest good also produces an inward transformation of our hearts that inclines us to seek the flourishing of the othered.[9]

8. Recall our discussion of Augustine's distinction between use and enjoyment in chapter 1. For further analysis, see Eric Gregory, *Politics and the Order of Love: An Augustinian Ethic of Democratic Citizenship* (University of Chicago Press, 2008), and Jennifer A. Herdt, "Empathy Beyond the In-Group: Stoic Universalism and Augustinian Neighbor-Love," *Philosophy, Theology and the Sciences* 2, no. 1 (2015): 63–88.

9. Using the word "othered" emphasizes that what makes someone the "other" is not anything inherent in themselves. No one is born "other." We are only *othered* when we do not fit systems of normativity and, at times, supremacy.

Loving our neighbors transforms our minds, hearts, desires, and actions precisely because it makes us acutely aware of the extent of God's divine love for us. Another way of saying this is that love begets love. When we intentionally practice loving our neighbors, we cultivate liturgies, rhythms, and habits that make us more prone to increasingly organic, unorganized practices of love. Love primes us to notice spaces, people, and places in need of love. When we love rightly, we can better perceive and respond to those around us.

This call to love is a call to become neighbors because, as Abhishiktananda writes, it opens our eyes to the unifying power of the Spirit where "no one can be a stranger to anyone else."[10] In other words, the work of becoming neighbors is simultaneously the work of no longer being strangers. It is the task of recognizing the image and work of God in another and cherishing that person as part of God's good creation. It is a movement toward others in and for the sake of love of both God and neighbor. As Abhishiktananda concludes: "Every human relationship is shot through with the Trinitarian mystery. God is everywhere, and God alone is everywhere, at the same time hidden and disclosed in his manifold self-manifestation. It is God, and only God, who gives, God who receives, God who loves, God who is loved."[11]

—

Traveling from Palestine, John Cassian, a fourth-century desert father, once visited a fellow Egyptian monk who welcomed him in for a meal. Although the monk was in a season of fasting, he sat down to share a meal with Cassian and his companions. Confused, Cassian asked the monk why he broke his fast. The monk replied, "Fasting is always possible, but I cannot keep you here forever. . . . God's law demands from us perfect love. I receive Christ when I

10. Abhishiktananda, *Prayer*, new ed. (Canterbury Press, 2006), 43.
11. Abhishiktananda, *Prayer*, 29.

receive you, so I must do all I can to show you love. When I have said goodbye to you, I can take up my rule of fasting again."[12]

This is neighbor love: welcoming and serving the stranger as if we were receiving Christ himself, even when it comes at a cost to ourselves.

A Call to Goodness

A second belief that we bring to the table is that God *is* good. The Scriptures are filled with this language: "Good and upright is the LORD" (Ps. 25:8); "The LORD is good" (Nah. 1:7); "The LORD is just in all his ways" (Ps. 145:17); "No one is good but God alone" (Mark 10:18). Jesus, too, places God's goodness at the core of God's divinity (Matt. 5:45; Luke 6:36).[13] The rhythms and liturgies of the church echo this. We sing about God's goodness in worship. We greet one another with the declaration that "God is good!," which is met with the reply, "All the time!" Every Sunday we bear witness to God's good work in our lives through our testimonies and prayers of thanksgiving.

When we say that God is good, though, we are not only describing an attribute of God. We are making a statement about God's nature: God is *the* good that lies behind all good things—including the common good. Translating Psalm 119:68, the Anglican theologian Oliver O'Donovan gives us a clunky but helpful phrase to describe this: God is "the good and good-ing one."[14]

12. Benedicta Ward, ed., *The Desert Fathers: Sayings of the Early Christian Monks* (Penguin Books, 2003), 134–35.

13. Andrew DeCort, *Blessed Are the Others: Jesus' Way in a Violent World* (BitterSweet Books, 2024), 66.

14. See Oliver O'Donovan, *The Disappearance of Ethics: The Gifford Lectures* (Eerdmans, 2024). Also his lecture "Good, Doing Good, and the Goods," YouTube, April 16, 2021, presented to the Henry Center at Trinity Evangelical University, https://tinyurl.com/y2b5trnb.

Another way to put it is this: God *is* what God *does*.[15] God's being and God's action cannot be separated. We know that God is good because God *is* what God *shares* with us. God does not simply hold goodness in Godself, doling it out sparsely. No, the apostle John beckons us in his first letter to "see what love the Father has given us, that we should be called children of God" (1 John 3:1). "We have known and believe the love that God has for us. God is love, and those who abide in love abide in God, and God abides in them" (1 John 4:16). God's goodness is revealed in both what is shared and the very act of sharing. We know God is good because of God's fundamental desire and movement toward community to bring justice and peace. God offers us the good and does so in abundance. O'Donovan draws a helpful image when he explains that we encounter the good not merely in a derivative way but in its source: "the good is met with" through this common life cultivated in the neighborhood and at the table.[16]

—

Theologians speak of Jesus Christ as the *logos incarnandus*: a God who was, is, and ever will be bound toward enfleshment.[17] Jesus is the goodness and love of God given to us—mysteriously united with the flesh and blood of creation. The incarnation is the intimate entrance of the Creator into the chaos, not to control it but to smell, touch, taste, see, heal, and love. Christ comes in the vulnerability of hope, offering a better way to be in this world for those who will

15. For more on the relationship between God's being and action, see Thomas Aquinas's writing on the "self-imparting good," the *bonum diffusivum sui*.

16. O'Donovan, "Good, Doing Good, and the Goods."

17. Bruce McCormack, "Grace and Being: The Role of God's Gracious Election in Karl Barth's Theological Ontology," in *The Cambridge Companion to Karl Barth*, ed. John Webster (Cambridge University Press, 2000), 94–95. For more on enfleshment, see M. Shawn Copeland, *Enfleshing Freedom: Body, Race, and Being* (Fortress, 2009).

listen. In the incarnation, we see God's desire to be local—to dwell in the neighborhood.

But why? Why does our good God come to us enfleshed? Why does God humble Godself to the form of creation? Why does God dive into the waves of cause and effect set in motion by God's very breath? Why does God desire a body that can be broken and bruised and demands nourishment and rest? Why does God choose to break bread and heal the sick with calloused hands? The answer is simple and profoundly beautiful: *to give it all away*.

God does not come to us because there was something for God to gain or prove to us. God comes to us in Jesus Christ so that we might gain God. Everything Jesus does is for the sake of others. Like God's act of creation, God builds, makes, and gives life so that creation can be enjoyed, not possessed. God does not come to dominate creation, forcing her to love the Creator. God comes to offer us an opportunity to experience the intimate joy of choosing to love God. Goodness exists to be given away.

The example of Christ is a model for us today as we seek the good of our neighbors, finding and giving goodness away just as Jesus did. We often assume that the work of seeking the common good is reserved for academics and politicians, activists and best-selling authors. We imagine that the work of cultivating this vision takes place in executive suites and boardrooms, Capitol buildings and the chambers of Congress. But Jesus's example tells us the opposite. To cast a vision of this common life, Christ does not take his message to the rulers and emperors of Rome, or pen a long treatise to be read in the halls of power. No, in his earthly ministry, the light of Christ revealed that goodness was present that the political powers and religious elites could not fathom: the undercommons.[18]

Jesus goes to the well in the heat of the day and offers a Samar-

18. For a deeper explanation of the "undercommons," see Stefano Harney and Fred Moten, *The Undercommons: Fugitive Planning and Black Study* (Minor Compositions, 2013).

itan woman the waters of eternal life (John 4). He beckons the tax collector Zacchaeus to come down from the sycamore tree and asks to share a meal with him (Luke 19). Before religious leaders enact violence, Jesus places his body between a woman caught in adultery and a stone-wielding crowd (John 8). Jesus draws near those deemed impure by Levitical law and reaches out his hand to touch and heal them (Mark 1; Luke 8). When a woman anoints Jesus's feet with expensive perfume, he reminds those angered by this act that he is preparing for his burial and that this woman will be remembered whenever his good news is proclaimed (Matt. 26). To find the goodness in our world, Jesus went to the margins of society to commune with people deemed impure. The first to hear Jesus's gospel of a kingdom to come were not those with tremendous influence and power but those humble enough to hear and respond.

Jesus, though, doesn't stop there. Echoing back to God's proclamation in Genesis, Jesus takes the ordinary things of our world and treats them as sacred and good. Truly, when asked about the deep things of God, Jesus does not look for an image or idea beyond our world. As the great poet and theologian Rubem Alves beautifully explains:

> We expected that he would talk about divine things. But he talks only about human things. Little ones. About the delights of heaven and the terrors of hell only a discreet murmur, if not silence. . . . He speaks of the tranquility of the birds, the beauty of the wild flowers, the sun that rises on the good and the evil, the rain, as well. And he tells us about children whose games are dancing and playing flutes; he goes to parties, introduces in the midst of the celebration his own wine; he speaks of purity of heart; points out that life is more important than laws; is saddened with our anguish, fear of the future, desire to run things and be seen, wish to be more important; he prefers the company of the marginal and the despised to the bowing and scraping of those who use sacred deodorants; he laughs at the powerful (even

> knowing its risks); rather the adulterer who sinned for love than those who, virtuous from age and from fear, stand with rocks in their hands; he eats and drinks with ordinary people, speaks in an enigmatic manner, knowing that pearls should not be cast before swine (to the pigs, slop); he tells frightful stories in which the villains of real life always appear as heroes and the heroes of real life always appear as villains. But these are things of this world, about men and women, children and old people, animals and trees. Right. He talks about our world. About life. About our bodies. He talks about smiles and tears.[19]

When asked, "Who are you?" Jesus does not answer us with long-winded theological jargon. Instead, Jesus speaks about his desires. "God is love. And he tells us about his dream of love. He places it alive, among us. Jesus of Nazareth is God's desire. He is his choice. A lovelier, more beautiful, more delightful thing there can not be."[20]

God's eternal work as the "good and gooding one" shapes how we cultivate and pursue a common good because, when we believe God is the source of all goodness, we can seek the good far beyond the banner of Christianity. In other words, God's goodness frees us to pursue the goodness found in both our neighbors, who possess and portray the image of God, and our world, which reflects the glory of God. Because we know that God's good presence lies behind all good things, we can locate goodness at the table where the common good is cultivated across religion, culture, and community. We can join God at the table where the sacred and good desire to listen, learn, serve, and dwell with our neighbors stirs in us. Like Christ, we can live into this holy curiosity toward our neighbors because they are worthy of our love and attention.

19. Rubem A. Alves, *I Believe in the Resurrection of the Body* (Wipf & Stock, 1986), 31–32.

20. Alves, *I Believe*, 33.

A Call to Community

A third belief that Christians offer to the table spread is the belief that God exists in Holy Trinity—an eternal relationship of Father, Son, and Spirit. As creatures made in the image of God, humans reflect this desire to belong and be known by others. We are made to exist in community.

This is why the church is central to the Christian life. It is not only a place where followers of Jesus are taught the deep things of God; it is a place where we are deeply formed by God and our neighbor.[21] As a living community, the church gathers those united in Jesus Christ to look not only vertically to God but also horizontally to one another. The church does not function like spokes on a wheel where each piece is connected to a shared hub but disconnected and spread in a different direction. The church is like a grand tapestry: lines of thread woven together holding and sustaining one another. Each thread depends on the integrity of the whole. This woven and interdependent structure is what makes tapestry beautiful, but it is also what makes it vulnerable. If one piece breaks, a process of fraying and undoing ensues. The integrity of each piece matters.

In the New Testament, the word used to describe this tapestry of community is *koinōnia*. This word, familiar to many Christians today, is derived from *koinos*, or "common."[22] Luke uses *koinōnia* to name the fellowship of the early church as they continued in the

21. The French sociologist Émile Durkheim argues that humans define themselves in relation to the groups they belong to. For Durkheim's in-depth evaluation of human social identity, see *The Elementary Forms of the Religious Life*, published in 1912.

22. In his letter to Titus, Paul opens with an appeal to the "faith we share" (1:4). Jude, similarly, grounds his exhortation to contend for the faith in the salvation shared by the apostle and his audience (Jude 3). *Koinos* is also used in the New Testament to describe what is general or ordinary and set in contrast to what is holy or set apart (Acts 10:14; Rom. 14:14; Heb. 10:29). However, the word extends beyond this specific use.

teachings of Jesus, the breaking of bread, and prayer (Acts 2:42). Paul, in his letters to the Corinthians, uses this language to name the act of communion both with the "blood of Christ" (1 Cor. 10:16) and with the Holy Spirit (2 Cor. 13:14). First John, too, is filled with descriptions of *koinōnia* fellowship (1:3–7).

Less familiar to Christians today is the active form *koinōnia* takes as it describes not only the community but the act of communication—of giving to and sharing with others. Paul uses *koinōnia* to describe both Christian fellowship (1 Cor. 1:9; Gal. 2:9; Eph. 3:9) and the contributions made for the church in Jerusalem (Rom. 15:26). In his letter to Philemon, Paul hopes that the "communication of faith" might be made effective (6 KJV). The author of Hebrews uses a verbal form of *koinōnia* when they instruct their readers to "not neglect to do good and to share what [they] have, for such sacrifices are pleasing to God" (13:16). Even in its infancy, the early church knew that following Christ meant believing things about God and participating in God's generous work in the neighborhood. Drawn from their reception of God's goodness, the early church was named and marked by a radical practice of giving.[23]

The call to community matters because community grounds and locates us. We are not aimless beings, existing above or outside of time.[24] The communities we place ourselves within profoundly shape our attitudes and actions. This community—whether social, familial, relational, professional, or otherwise—instills and reaf-

23. Oliver O'Donovan explains that the logic of communication "is summed up in the phrase: 'what is "mine" is "ours."' Not 'what is "mine" is "yours,"' which is the logic of bestowal, nor 'this "mine" is yours, and this "yours" is mine,' which is the logic of exchange." For the Christian, God's divine act of communication wraps us up in the life of God, drawing us into the divine, eternal communion of God. This communication is a crucial and fundamental act of God as Jesus Christ—through his incarnation, life, death, resurrection, and ascension—communicates the merits of God onto us. Oliver O'Donovan, *Entering into Rest: Theology as Ethics*, vol. 3 (Eerdmans, 2017), 48.

24. See James K. A. Smith, *How to Inhabit Time: Understanding the Past, Facing the Future, Living Faithfully Now* (Baker Books, 2022).

firms the value systems and beliefs we hold true, and places practices around those beliefs to affirm them.

When we begin to believe we can exist apart from such influences, we become unreliable narrators of our own lives, unable to see the broader context in which we live. It's like someone who jumps out of a plane and says, "I'm flying!" It takes a broader community to warn them, "No, you're falling! Pull the parachute!" Or think of an alcoholic isolated in their addiction. On their own, they might say, "I'm fine, really!" Only in community can a trusted friend say, "No, you're not. Let me get you help." It is no wonder that inpatient care for those embracing false stories about themselves often includes group therapy—a community that can detox, reconfigure, and ground one's imagination.

For followers of Christ, *koinōnia* points to a grounded, located community seeking to live into the spiritual reality of Jesus's prayer that the church may be one just as Christ and the Father are one (John 17:21). It is an active practice of being together *as* communion in a specific place and time.[25] To do this, the church joined arm in arm and began walking through life together. It was not enough to individually follow Jesus on their own route. To forge a true community, the first believers looked to their neighbors and began to plot out a path to sojourn through.

—

"Maybe redemption is not a place you find," writes John West, "but a system of mapmaking. Sketch a land. Pencil in dragons. Imagine it real, resplendent, and broken under a waxing moon."[26] The early church understood this. Their cartography included not only seeing and hearing the world but tasting, smelling, and touching it. Their *koinōnia* fellowship was marked by loving embrace and the Eucharist meal.

25. See John D. Zizioulas, *Being as Communion: Studies in Personhood and the Church* (St. Vladimir's Seminary Press, 1985).

26. John West, *Lessons and Carols: A Meditation on Recovery* (Eerdmans, 2023), 138.

When we come to the common table today, we bring the routes we take and the paths we've created to craft a system of maps leading toward the flourishing of our whole community. These map markings are the rituals, myths, customs, traditions, and experiences of our communities. For Christians, these well-traveled paths are marked by Christians living out our calling to love our neighbors, seek goodness in this world, and build communities of belonging.

When we consider our pursuit of the common good, we must think deeply about who is included in that first word: the *commons*, the community. The type of good community that God is calling us to cultivate is expansive and freeing. God is drawing us to shared spaces where we can love our neighbors radically and unconditionally. The triune God is beckoning us to build communities of belonging where we are joined together across our differences in a shared pursuit of happiness and flourishing.

God is calling us, again and again, to the table.

The Potluck

Eboo was right. The table where the common good is cultivated is a potluck.[27] Unlike the "great American melting pot," where all of our particular languages, cultures, values, beliefs, and cuisines are tossed into a giant vat and churned into a bland chum, the potluck is an invitation to craft a dish that is meaningful to you and then offer it to others to be eaten alongside a dish that is meaningful to your neighbor.

The potluck helps illustrate the participatory nature of the table. As we discussed in the last chapter, Christians are often eager to play host but reluctant to sit as guests at the table of another. The potluck positions the meal in a communally owned space where all who gather are both host and guest, both givers and receivers. This

27. See my article "The Great American Potluck," *Sojourners*, October 11, 2021, https://tinyurl.com/335vsaz5. Also Danielle Allen, *Talking to Strangers: Anxieties of Citizenship Since Brown v. Board of Education* (University of Chicago Press, 2004), and Patel, *Out of Many Faiths*.

dynamic demonstrates the power of pluralism, which welcomes the presence of deep difference as an opportunity to engage and celebrate the diversity present all around us.

Every dish at the potluck contains the stories, beliefs, and histories of the neighbor who made it. What is incredible about the potluck is that, when we eat these dishes alongside one another, each dish tastes different from when it's eaten alone. The biriyani I bring will taste different when my neighbor's empanada precedes it, and the cold beet soup that follows will undoubtedly be impacted by the *kasuri methi* and *haldi* that hang on the tongue after a bite of saffron-stained rice. When our "dishes" are eaten together, we taste them anew.

Of course, no potluck is perfect. While the invitation to join in this great community feast may be open to all, the context of our gathering matters. If we host this gathering in a location far from any public transportation routes, how will those without a vehicle be able to join? If the event is on Saturday morning, how will our Shabbat-observing neighbors participate? If the local megachurch hosts the neighborhood potluck every week because they have a large meeting space and an industrial fridge to hold the food, how will the attendees from the nearby gurdwara and masjid ever feel like they have shared ownership of this meal?

Even more, in our current social and political climate, we must reckon with a troubling scenario: What if someone tries to bring poison to the potluck? While this is a grim question, it is also a realistic one. In our world, there are those who actively hate and seek the harm of others. Because of the malice, prejudice, and fear in our world, there are opportunistic and vengeful individuals who will exploit this sacred space to inflict harm. We cannot pretend such hateful action is an abstract, distant reality.

Does this mean we should not gather or eat together? By no means. However, we must recognize that the potluck is not unconsidered, wishful thinking. It is strategic. All are welcome, but community guidelines are established. The door is open wide, and there is a volunteer present to greet each guest. For the sake of our neighbors—especially marginalized, disenfranchised, immunocompromised, disabled, and minoritized neighbors—we must also consider the boundary lines we will draw to keep our community safe and free to flourish. These actions are not about exclusion; they're about care. We join in this work with a desire to know and be known, to love and love others in a space where we can be fully present.

—

To join in cultivating a common good, we must recognize that any meaningful vision of this common life will bind our flourishing with the flourishing of our neighbors. Theory and theology proposed from a distance will do little for us as we cultivate localized visions of the common good. Instead, we need tangible, neighborhood-driven theology that speaks to the deep stories we tell about ourselves and the world around us. We need lived theologies that recognize our experience, embrace our particular context, and lead us to a meaningful conception of the common good. We must take what we believe about God and place it on the ground as we live out our calling to love, goodness, and community.

The common good begins by finding God at work in the neighborhood as we come to the shared table and feast together. Ultimately, this shared meal turns us toward an expansive vision of the neighborhood. This telos of the shared table and the practice of neighboring is a deeply hopeful one. It centers the loving touch shared among a community and the sense of being valued and cared for. It recognizes that we are most creative and imaginative when we love because it is love that draws us out of ourselves and toward the cares and concerns of others.[28] Our good and gooding God is active and working in the world today. This redemptive and sacred work cannot be contained in a single place or people. Our incredible, God-given task is to join God in it as we seek this good in and for our community through radical practices of neighbor love.

28. See Kenda Creasy Dean, *Innovating for Love: Joining God's Expedition Through Christian Social Innovation* (Market Square Publishing, 2022).

3

THE PRACTICES OF NEIGHBOR LOVE

"Every human being is neighbor to every other human being. Ask nature, is he unknown? He's human. Is she an enemy? She's human. Is he a foe? He's human. Is she a friend? Let her stay a friend. Is he an enemy? Let him become a friend."

—Augustine, Sermon 299D, in *Sermons: III/8 (273–305A) on the Saints*

"God is present wherever genuine love is present, or perhaps more accurately, God, who is omnipresent but often experienced as absence, is made available through the expression of genuine love. The life of God and the life of humans are for this one time and in this one way-one thing."

—Christian Wiman, *He Held Radical Light: The Art of Faith, the Faith of Art*

The sacred and enduring task of loving our neighbor seems simple enough. Love is something we (hopefully) all share and receive. No matter if we have the philosophical and theological jargon to describe it, we are all acquainted with love and the multitude of ways it is expressed, directed, and received. For example, I love my partner, my parents, a sunny day, and the Green Bay Packers. But each of these loves is expressed through different practices. I love Emily by finding small ways to bring her joy each day. I love my parents by expressing gratitude for the blessing they've been in my life. I love a sunny day by wishing for its presence and then spending the day outside. I love the Green Bay Packers by courageously donning my green and gold apparel when I am in Chicago.

When it comes to loving our neighbors, though, we often fail to have tangible practices in mind of how our love might be expressed. How do I love my neighbor across the street whose house is adorned with American flags and MAGA signs? Does that differ from how I love my neighbor with a multicolored Pride flag? How do I love the unhoused person who often stands at the highway exit on my route home? How do I love the barista at my local coffee shop who consistently provides me with a delicious cortado? How do I love my undocumented neighbor struggling to find work? How do I love the pastor down the road who pours her heart and soul out every Sunday?

There is no single answer to any of these questions because we all have different neighbors who need to be loved in particular ways. However, there are undoubtedly similarities between your neighbors and mine. Looking back on the long-standing and tested ways that followers of Jesus have worked toward the good of their neighbors, certain practices of love appear across place and time. I find these practices significant because, as we intentionally incorporate them into our lives, they become part of our very being. In other words, these practices of neighbor love form us toward the divine love of God so deeply that, over time, we begin to act out of this posture without hesitation.[1]

Christian faith is not merely held intellectually in our minds. It is woven into our body and soul. When faith is lived out through the practices of neighbor love, we become people who not only show compassion but are compassionate, who not only demonstrate humility but are humble, who not only struggle for justice but are just. I believe that if we can show up to the table embodying these practices, we can meaningfully contribute to the shared work of seeking the common good while also bearing witness to our good, loving, and triune God.

Compassion

There are few better places to understand compassion than the parable of the Good Samaritan. Bringing life to his command to love God and neighbor, Jesus tells the story of a man robbed by thieves, beaten, and left for dead on the side of the road. As he lies dying, both a priest and a Levite pass the man by on the other side of the road without offering help. However, a Samaritan traveling this path between Jerusalem and Jericho perceives this man in need and is "moved with compassion" (Luke 10:33). The Samaritan treats the

1. As Ashish Varma writes, "The call to life in Christ is the call to excellence according to the purposes of God in Christ by the Spirit. Beyond human flourishing in a natural sense—though it is not discounted—life in Christ is the call toward excellent fellowship with God and, by connection, with the fellow creatures of God." "Jews and Gentiles Together in Christ? The Jerusalem Council on Racial Reconciliation," *Ex Auditu* 33 (2017): 156.

man's wounds, places him on his animal, takes him to an inn, and cares for him.

The Greek word that Luke uses to describe compassion—*splagchnizomai*—helps us understand why this response led the Samaritan to drop everything and help. Unlike pity, which implies a position of condescension, *splagchnizomai* describes the moral and spiritual compulsion to feel the pain of others and come alongside them in a moment of need. It, quite literally, describes the turning in one's inner parts. The Samaritan did not have pity; he had compassion. His stomach churned at the reminder of a world marred with violence and injustice.

This parable offers us an example of compassionate neighbor love marked by mutuality and responsibility, not condescension and cowardice. Jesus's choice to make a Samaritan the protagonist of this parable set a standard for how his followers were expected to act in the world. The outcast, marginalized, stereotyped, and disenfranchised Samaritan had every excuse to care for his own needs. Certainly, the systems of power and privilege that may have created the robbers in the first place were not his fault. Even still, it was the Samaritan man who stopped to care for the man in need, offering him what he had at that moment and investing himself in the robbed man's long-term well-being.[2]

There are countless implications and lessons contained within this parable. I will highlight only three. First, the Samaritan shows us that we are called to radical compassion, even when we are not the ones who caused harm or committed the wrongdoing. As cries of injustice and wrongdoing are heard clearly today, there is a temptation to keep the struggles of our neighbors at a distance. Rather than getting caught up in the messiness of systemic oppression, food apartheid, police brutality, and housing inequity, we pass by like the priest and Levite who witness the harm done but excuse the man on

2. See Nicholas Wolterstorff, *Justice: Rights and Wrongs* (Princeton University Press, 2010), 217–18.

the road as someone else's problem. Christians, though, are called to participate in the work of healing. The Samaritan had little concern about who committed violence against the man beaten and robbed on the road. Simply witnessing someone in need was enough to move him toward action.

Second, this parable fuses neighbor love with *enemy* love. If Christians know anything about the historical context of this passage, it is often that the Jewish people and the Samaritans were irreparably at odds. The common title of this parable (which was never spoken by Jesus) points to this: a *good* Samaritan is an oxymoron because it is assumed that the collective and common character of the "Samaritan" is flawed.[3] It would be one thing, perhaps even predictable, for Jesus to position the Samaritan as the one beaten and left for dead and place the priest or Levite as the one who lends a compassionate hand. This would certainly be a practice of enemy love. But Jesus takes his Jewish audience a step further by displacing them as the protagonist of the story. In doing so, he challenges the limits of their moral imagination by asking not only if they could have love for their enemy but if they could imagine their enemy loving them back.

Finally, we see in this story that the command to love our neighbor often means that we are loving *strangers*. This harkens back to the first command to love one's neighbor found in the Levitical law: "When an alien resides with you in your land, you shall not oppress the alien. The alien who resides with you shall be to you as the native-born among you; you shall love the alien as yourself, for you were aliens in the land of Egypt: I am the Lord your God" (Lev. 19:33–34). When we think of our neighbors, we might first think of our friend three doors down who comes over once a week for dinner. But those encompassed within this category of "neighbor" go far beyond that.

3. Andrew T. Draper, *A Theology of Race and Place: Liberation and Reconciliation in the Works of Jennings and Carter* (Pickwick, 2016), 274.

In his popular *The Message* translation of the New Testament, Eugene Peterson reframes Jesus's concluding question to the lawyer who had initially asked for clarification as to *who* his neighbor was: "What do you think?" Jesus asks. "Which of the three became a neighbor to the man attacked by robbers?" (Luke 10:36 *The Message*). Peterson's translation stands out from others by emphasizing Jesus's point: the designation of "neighbor" has less to do with location and more to do with a disposition of loving, compassionate action. As Jesus promises, "Blessed are the compassionate, for they will be mirrored with compassion" (Matt. 5:7).[4]

Humility

In his book *Being and Time*, the philosopher Martin Heidegger identifies the experience of "thrownness."[5] This language aptly describes the experience: a sense of being tossed into the world like a rock down a steep forest slope, knocking against trees and hurling through thick brush. Thrownness is the humbling moment we become aware of all the countless forces and choices that act upon us. It arises when we stop and ask ourselves, "How did I get here?" It is the realization that we are *who* we are because of the people around us and the places we exist.

Thrownness, though, goes two ways. We are not only thrown; we are also throwers. As the world acts upon us, we also act upon the world. By interacting with others, we become one of many forces that our friends and neighbors recognize in their own experience

4. Andrew DeCort translates the Greek word *eleémōn* in this verse as "compassionate" in *Blessed Are the Others: Jesus' Way in a Violent World* (BitterSweet Books, 2024), 98.

5. See Martin Heidegger, *Being and Time*, trans. John Macquarrie and Edward Robinson (Harper Perennial Modern Classics, 2008). My reading of Heidegger's concept of "thrownness" is informed and influenced by James K. A. Smith and his book *How to Inhabit Time: Understanding the Past, Facing the Future, Living Faithfully Now* (Baker Books, 2022).

of thrownness. There is relational reciprocity here of giving and receiving, of acting and being acted upon. Thrownness reminds us that we are always dependent on our environment, never above or beyond its formative power. We are enmeshed in tangled webs of interdependence where we, at once, are being formed and are forming others. Recognizing our thrownness humbles us.

This is why I find the incarnation deeply moving. God, the original and ultimate "thrower," enters into the thrownness of the world. Rather than standing outside the waves and ripples of cause and effect, Jesus enters the rotations of a world that he set in motion. Christ exists as both creator and creation, divine and human. Christ does not come to us in a cloud of glory or place himself on an earthly throne. Instead, Jesus humbles himself into Mary's womb and is birthed into the world he created at the beginning of time. He places himself in John's arms and is plunged into the Jordan River. He empties himself in taking human likeness and walks with his creation even to the point of death (Phil. 2:7–8). God so intimately enters this world that the world is transformed by God's touch, and God, in return, is moved by the world. Christian Wiman puts it simply: Christ is contingent.[6]

Christ's contingency should humble us, too. In a world that prioritizes individualism and uplifts self-autonomy, Christ chooses to become dependent upon creation—upon oxygen in his lungs and food in his stomach, upon friendships to nourish his soul and human feet to carry forth the gospel into the world. Christ is wrapped up with creation so intimately that he weeps and mourns at the death of his friend Lazarus. He grows tired and weary after a long day. Righteous fury boils within him when he sees houses of worship used for profit or human beings maligned and abused. Jesus also laughs and entertains his friends. He dances and sings at a wedding feast after turning water into the sweetest wine. He places his human

6. Christian Wiman, *My Bright Abyss: Meditation of a Modern Believer* (Farrar, Straus & Giroux, 2013), 16–17.

body between people in need and those ready to throw stones. He takes time to sit with the children and the least, teaching that the kingdom of God belongs to them. God humbles himself to be with us—and does so at the greatest cost to himself.

Years ago, a wise professor named Michael McDuffee taught me something about humility that I will never forget: "God permits himself to be a question mark in the mind of those he has created by his own hand. This is the greatest act of humility the world will ever know. How far will you descend? How far will you rise? You can do neither more than God himself. Who is exalted on high and the lowest of servants." Humility is the sapling that grows out of the recognition that we are not our own; we are bound to one another. Our roots are dug into the same earth. Loving our neighbors in humility recognizes the countless ways we belong to one another and are molded by the people around us. It follows the example of God in Jesus Christ, who descends from the heavens to encounter the world enfleshed. When we come to the table in humility, we acknowledge that our lives are intertwined with our neighbors. Our flourishing is wrapped up with theirs.[7]

Translation

In the context of neighbor love, translation is the work of making ideas and concepts understandable across communities. Think of those who speak multiple languages. To translate between two languages takes far more than exchanging one word for another. It is a complex process that involves two different vocabularies, grammars, cultural norms, idioms, inflections, cadences, and more. Translators are builders who use their bilingual, bicultural knowledge to bridge communities together across lines of difference.

7. True humility erupts from the daily practice of remembering that "we are participating, at Christ's invitation, in redemption that God already has well underway." Kenda Creasy Dean, *Innovating for Love: Joining God's Expedition Through Christian Social Innovation* (Market Square Publishing, 2022), 43.

All Christians are called to the work of translation. As children of God, we stand in the space between heaven and earth, ascension and return, "already" and "not yet." By the power of the Holy Spirit, we have the eyes to see the kingdom of God breaking into the lived reality of everyday life: in the breaking of bread and sharing of wine in Communion, in the ladles filled with soup at a food pantry, in the hug embraced between a parent and a child. As we seek the common good in our communities, it is our task to translate—to make known—God's presence to those who cannot yet see God at work in the world.

Anyone who has tried to learn a new language knows that mobile apps and online tutorials can only take you so far. At some point, you must make the leap into conversing with someone fluent in the language you're trying to learn. If you want true fluency, you must go even further and spend time immersed in that language. As gospel translators, we often take the language app approach: "Here is what you need to know to be saved." "Learn and say these specific words and you will be a Christian." Loving our neighbors in this way does very little good. Instead, our invitation is into conversation: "Come and learn how we speak! See if these words, concepts, idioms, and ideas (and the stories we tell through them) help you make meaning of the world."[8] Bringing Christianity to the table of the common good is an invitation for others to immerse themselves in the Christian tradition and experience living with the resurrected imagination of Christ.

In my experience, this work of translation is both challenging and humbling. In the year leading up to the 2020 election, I worked as a research assistant to Asma Uddin, a Muslim attorney and public scholar, as she wrote a book on Muslims and evangelicals.[9] Every day, Asma would send me articles about how evangelicals

8. James K. A. Smith, *Who's Afraid of Relativism: Community, Contingency, and Creaturehood* (Baker Academic, 2014), 175.

9. See Asma Uddin, *The Politics of Vulnerability: How to Heal Muslim-Christian Relations in a Post-Christian America* (Pegasus Books, 2021).

were conducting themselves and ask for me to explain why these Christians acted in ways that betrayed the very virtues and values they espoused. When Asma first began posing these questions, I'd answer them as I'd answer another Christian. I used my theological vocabulary and insider language ("Christian-eese" is what we would call it in youth group) to explain these events. Asma, who is a brilliant scholar, did not have a clue what I was saying.[10]

I quickly realized that, to be of any help, I'd have to translate these evangelical concepts, ideas, and vulnerabilities into language, illustrations, and concepts that we could both understand as people deeply rooted in different faith traditions. Together, we parsed through evangelical action in a way that Asma could better understand through examining the historical context, decoding language, and placing the evangelical tradition within the broader practice of Christianity in America. What made our collaboration fruitful was the recognition of this "language" barrier and shared investment in translating concepts across our traditions.

My work with Asma is just one example of why translation is both a work of neighbor love and a necessity for the work of seeking the common good. Translation invites others to understand how we think and engage in the world beyond identity labels that box us into certain expectations. Good translators reveal how cross-cultural communication is possible and that a vision of shared community

10. This example also highlights how communities are essential to how we understand ourselves and the world around us. Communities not only instill and reaffirm in us value systems, beliefs, and the practices that are drawn from them, the formation of communities also shapes the very way that we interpret the words that we hear. When words like "democracy," "social justice," or "freedom" are used in different contexts, they mean different things; and perhaps more importantly, they assume different consequences. The German philosopher Ludwig Wittgenstein calls this the "language game": Words, when employed in different communities of practice, lead to different ends. Meaning is not fixed, it is dynamic. See Wittgenstein's *Philosophical Investigations*, published posthumously in 1953.

and belonging amid our differences is well within our grasp. Translation reveals that the walls constructed to separate communities can easily crumble, making way for a shared table.

Resonance

Resonance describes the pleasing sound of instruments in tune, of musicians mirroring one another's sound waves. Think, for example, of a large orchestra. If you attend a concert, you will hear the musicians tune their instruments before they begin playing. While there are digital devices that can perfectly "tune" an instrument, these musicians do not each individually pull out their personal tuner. Instead, a note is given and, section by section, each player aligns their instrument's pitch to those next to them. By adjusting valves, knobs, and mouthpieces, each instrumentalist shapes the sound coming from their instrument to align with the broader group. It doesn't matter if their tuning matches the machine-generated answer. What is important is that each musician is attuned to each other.

Neighbor love looks a lot like this pursuit of resonance. To love our neighbors is to attune ourselves to their pitch, matching their tone—whether that be cries of joy or sorrow—as we join together in a harmonious melody of flourishing. This is not a onetime event. It is an ongoing task. While a band may tune together at the beginning of a performance, instruments will slowly shrink, expand, and bend in different ways. Great musicians are never only playing; they are actively listening to others and making subtle adjustments to align themselves with the greater sound. Resonance requires the presence of many voices and instruments that are, at once, contributing their part and listening to the whole.

In his book *Resonance: A Sociology of Our Relationship to the World*, Hartmut Rosa explains how the entire quality of our existence is tied to our relationship to, or resonance with, the world.[11] Our imagina-

11. Hartmut Rosa, *Resonance: A Sociology of Our Relationship to the World*,

tions are shaped by and through our relationship with the people around us, our society, and the earth beneath our feet. When we resonate with our neighbors—mutually attuned to each other's fears, vulnerabilities, desires, and loves—we can foster a community where we can mutually flourish through practices of attention and empathy.

Rosa sets resonance in contrast to alienation, which is a way of relating to the world absent of a response.[12] The relational echolocation waves are sent out in search of connection, but they are not returned. If community, as we discussed in chapter 2, provides us with a context and a sense of being grounded in time, then the experience of alienation is the opposite: alienation suspends and freezes us in time. We feel disconnected from the past, future, and present—including the people, places, and things they contain. The world is marked by shades of gray and a sense of dullness. In short, it is an acute sense of unbelonging.

As we navigate the current "loneliness epidemic," this experience of alienation is an intimate reality for many people.[13] This is why resonance matters decisively as a practice of neighbor love. Norman Wirzba rightly summarizes that "When resonance is happening, people are in tune with each other and appreciate that their own well-being is intimately bound up with the well-being of others."[14] When we hold loving, resonant relationships with those at the table, our movement in and through our community is marked by

---

trans. James C. Wagner (Polity, 2019). I first learned of Rosa's work through Norman Wirzba's book *Love's Braided Dance: Hope in a Time of Crisis* (Yale University Press, 2024), where he brings resonance into conversation with hope.

12. In Rosa's words, "Alienation denotes a specific form of relationship to the world in which subject and world confront each other with indifference or hostility (repulsion) and thus without any inner connection." *Resonance*, 184.

13. See "Our Epidemic of Loneliness and Isolation," U.S. Surgeon General's Advisory on the Healing Effects of Social Connection and Community, 2023, https://tinyurl.com/46j626r3.

14. Wirzba, *Love's Braided Dance*, 53.

a recognition that we are all playing the same communal song of flourishing and well-being. We are part of a common orchestra. As attentive neighbors, we can sense when alienation and dissonance are present and respond with love.

Lamentation

Lament is the sacred work of responding to the disorienting and overwhelming experience of suffering. It is also a loving act of protest and proclamation. It draws us to work toward the common good by first acknowledging the presence of evil and injustice and then beckoning a God who knows our suffering to make things right.

As an individual practice, lamentation provides the freedom to share our grievances with God, who intimately knows the pain of suffering. The psalms are filled with these refrains: *How long, O Lord? Will you forget me forever? . . . How long must I bear pain in my soul and have sorrow in my heart all day long?* In doing so, we place our suffering within the greater context of God's purposes for us. This does not diminish or negate our pain, but it gives us reason for hope.

As a communal practice, lament helps us carry the burdens of our neighbors. When lamentation is shared, those suffering are bound up in a community of support who can cry out to God alongside them. The shared practice of lament also helps those who mourn endure the present moment. There is something about sharing in suffering—about collectively acknowledging that we live in a world marked by loss, evil, injustice, and pain—that makes our suffering more bearable. There is an incredible power in having one's grief seen and validated.[15]

15. "To speak extreme grief," writes Christian Wiman, "is to mark it as a thing that *can be spoken of*. It is to bring the abyss into the realm of consciousness; perhaps not into the realm of meaning, which would be to deform and falsely diminish it. But into the realm of time, which implies, if nothing else, the possibility of change." Christian Wiman, *Zero at the Bone: Fifty Entries Against Despair* (Farrar, Straus & Giroux, 2023), 48.

The book of Lamentations provides an in-depth look into this mourning practice. Written primarily by Jeremiah after the fall and destruction of Jerusalem, this prophetic book collects and records the communal voice of a defeated and destroyed Jerusalem told by her people—enslaved and colonized, deserted and widowed. As the Hebrew title of the book, *'ekhah*, reveals, the people of Israel cry out to God: "How!?"[16] Lamentations is filled with such cries of anguish as Jeremiah reaches into the depths of his pain to offer us a glimpse into his agonizing emotions of loss, grief, and heartbreak. The poetic style in Hebrew intentionally even emulates a funeral dirge or elegy. The book of Lamentations does not gloss over suffering or explain it away; it embraces it. Jeremiah weeps and cannot turn his eyes away from the destruction around him.

This prophetic mourning teaches us that lamentation is both a recognition of and a response to a world that is not as it should be. As we pursue a common good with and for our neighbors, lamentation helps us rightly feel the weight of all that is wrong in our neighborhoods. As an active practice, though, lament does not paralyze us as we are crushed by the weight of the world. Instead, lament protests against our suffering. "To suffer in the face of some circumstance," says theologian Kevin Hector, "is to suffer *against* it, to endure it as that which should not be, and, so, as that which should be opposed."[17] In other words, the authentic and raw existence of suffering, grief, and anguish testifies to the presence of love in one's life. In this way, lamentation is an act of radical hope that God is present and will respond to us in such times of need. Lamentation reminds us that we cannot prophesy hope if we have never known despair. As Edgar reminds us in *King Lear*, "The worst is not so long as we can say, 'This is the worst.'"[18]

16. Soong-Chan Rah, *Prophetic Lament: A Call for Justice in Troubled Times* (InterVarsity Press, 2015), 45.

17. Kevin W. Hector, *Christianity as a Way of Life: A Systematic Theology* (Yale University Press, 2023), 193.

18. "[Edgar's] words suggest that even here, where life is so excruciating that our only surviving desire is to leave it, there is still a possibility for change.

Accompaniment

"To accompany someone is to go somewhere with [them], to break bread together, to be present on a journey with a beginning and an end."[19] The global health pioneer Dr. Paul Farmer dedicated his life to the spiritual work of accompaniment. In his early twenties, Dr. Farmer traveled to Haiti, where he witnessed people dying from preventable and curable diseases simply because they lacked access to basic medical care and clean drinking water. Wholly dissatisfied with the excuse that such poverty was impossible to overcome because resources were too scarce, Paul was filled with the kind of righteous indignation that does not allow you to sit still. Although he returned to the United States to attend Harvard Medical School, he spent his education and medical training traveling back and forth between Haiti and Massachusetts, taking what he gained in school—both knowledge and supplies—and serving the Haitian people.

In the early 1980s, Dr. Farmer cofounded a community-based health project, which eventually blossomed into a state-of-the-art hospital that doctors from around the globe still travel to serve. Several years after building this first clinic, Paul helped found Partners in Health (PIH) in 1987. In its short life, PIH has already expanded these public health efforts in Africa, Peru, Russia, Mexico, and the indigenous American Navajo Nation. Paul, too, spent his life traveling the world for PIH and special appointments while also serving as a professor of medical anthropology at Harvard.

Born out of his friendship with the liberation theologian Gustavo Gutiérrez, Dr. Farmer's practice of accompaniment was a living response to Gutiérrez's question of how we can show those struggling under the structures of violence, injustice, and poverty

---

And where there is even a possibility for change, there is hope." Wiman, *Zero at the Bone*, 48.

19. I am grateful to Dr. Annah Kuriakose for introducing me to Paul Farmer's work, including his conversations with Gutiérrez. Paul Farmer, *To Repair the World: Paul Farmer Speaks to the Next Generation*, ed. Jonathan L. Weigel (University of California Press, 2013), 234.

that God loves them.[20] No matter where he was in the world, Paul's practice of accompaniment often looked less like conversations in a hospital room and more like traveling long distances across difficult terrain to be with his patients in their homes and among their communities. Dr. Farmer did not want to just rid his patients of an ailment or disease. He felt the moral and ethical responsibility to understand the urgent circumstances of his patients' lives and remain with them through their healing.

Paul's longtime friend and biographer, Jennie Block, explains that the word "accompaniment," like the word "companion," comes from the Latin *cum pane*, which means "with bread." Accompaniment "implies sharing together, eating together, nourishing each other, walking together. The one who accompanies is like a midwife, helping us to come to life to live more fully."[21] To be a companion is to enter loving relationship with our neighbors—especially our poor, disenfranchised, heavy-laden, and pressed-down neighbors—for the long haul. "The companion," writes Dr. Farmer, says, "I'll go with you and support you on your journey wherever it leads. I'll keep you company and share your fate for a while—and by 'a while,' I don't mean 'a little while.' Accompaniment is about sticking with a task until it's deemed complete—not by the [companion] but by the person being accompanied."[22]

Accompaniment cannot be done from a distance. Carrying one another's burdens in a loving kinship means showing up to lift with real hands, not distant thoughts and prayers. It requires attention to and concern for the experience and needs of our neighbors. It takes form through the daily ministry of showing up, listening, conversing, celebrating, lamenting, feasting, and worshiping. It engages not

20. Paul Farmer and Gustavo Gutiérrez, *In the Company of the Poor: Conversations with Dr. Paul Farmer and Fr. Gustavo Gutiérrez*, ed. Michael Griffin and Jennie Weiss Block (Orbis Books, 2013), 27.

21. Jennie Weiss Block, *Paul Farmer: Servant to the Poor* (Liturgical Press, 2018), 151.

22. Farmer, *To Repair the World*, 234.

only our physical well-being but also our mental health, spiritual life, social location, financial situation, and moral vision.

When we take up the spiritual practice of accompaniment, we will find God in the most unexpected places and people. This practice makes real the wonderful reality that we are not all the same and, therefore, have much to learn from one another.[23] Following the great proclamation of "Immanuel," God with us, accompaniment raises in us a conviction that God is also with *them*. God is with the neighbor across the street, across the aisle, across the picket line, and across the world in Palestine or Sudan. God is present with those on the other side of the table where the common good is cultivated. God is with us, here and now, guiding our hearts and minds toward the flourishing of all creation.

23. John J. Thatamanil argues that if we are all fundamentally the same, then we have nothing to learn from one another. Our inclination toward curiosity is squashed. Curiosity is driven by the recognition that we are not the same. See *Circling the Elephant: A Comparative Theology of Religious Diversity* (Fordham University Press, 2020).

4

A COMMUNITY OF BUILDERS

"When people make good and beautiful things, they affirm that this world is worthy of our attention, love, and skill. I call this task humanity's enduring sacred vocation."

—Norman Wirzba,
This Sacred Life: Humanity's Place in a Wounded World

". . . to serve as a paradigm
now of what a plausible Future might be
is what we're here for."

—W. H. Auden, "The Garrison"

Christ's followers are called to build because our God is a builder. Created and creative in the image of God, we are tasked with creating good and beautiful things that serve those around us.[1] Whether it is a small business or a community garden, building together can accomplish far more than any individual effort. There is world-shaping power in building together toward belonging and the common good.

In his *Institutes*, John Calvin draws from the Scriptures to identify three "offices" that Jesus holds as he builds the first community of believers: prophet, priest, and king. As prophet, Christ is both the messenger and the message proclaimed. As priest, he is both the one who demands a sacrifice and the sacrificed element. As king, Christ is both the victor and the victory. These offices serve as prototypes for how Christians can engage in the world as followers and emulators of Christ.[2]

1. See Katherine M. Douglass, *Creative in the Image of God: An Aesthetic Practical Theology of Young Adult Faith* (Cascade, 2020).

2. John Calvin offers his treatment of the person and work of Christ in book 2 of his *Institutes*, giving three chapters to each (12 through 17). He also uses this framework in his Genevan Catechism (1545). What is helpful about Calvin is that his concern is not primarily about ontological questions for their own sake, but rather practical, soteriological ones. In other words, Calvin wants to know how Jesus's role as mediator *works*—what constitutes this role? My short outline here of Christ's prophetic, priestly, and kingly roles is adapted from Dr. Ashish Varma's systematic theology lectures shared through personal correspondence.

As Jesus models, these three roles are never neatly separated: He tells parables as a prophet, carries his cross to Golgotha as a priest, and resurrects as a king. However, each action is powerful and effective because of the others. The same can be said of Christ followers today. In different times and circumstances, we will live out all these roles, often simultaneously. By emulating Christ in these three ways, we can build new spaces of belonging, develop new ways to serve our communities, design new venues for humans to flourish, and lead the way in working toward a common good.[3]

The Prophet and the Public Square

Those who take up the mantle of a prophet in our world today reside in the public square and boldly speak truth to power. Attuned to God's presence in the world, the prophet both names how the world is not as it should be and casts a vision for the world as it *might* be—a world that God desires for us. Although prophets are often thought of as foretellers who predict the future, we find throughout the Bible that the prophet's primary task is actually forth-telling (proclaiming). The prophet is not a seer or fortune-teller. Their task is to bear witness to God's good desire for the world. The prophet possesses a moral imagination—an encompassing vision of how the world *ought* to be—and calls their community to follow in it.

In a cultural moment flooded with protest and activism, this work of prophecy is often coveted. However, the sacred work of the prophet is not one to take lightly. Those who stand on the front lines of marches and organize community efforts against injustice and inequality will soon tell you that this was not the path they desired, but it is the one demanded by the conditions of our world. If we look at the lives of ancient Israel's prophets or the life of Christ,

3. These categories are each named in their masculine form because they are proposed in relation to Christ's earthly ministry. However, they are unequivocally not gender-bound.

we will soon find that neither were given wealth and social prestige. They were reviled and often spent their days lamenting, fasting, and awaiting God's intervention. The Old Testament scholar Walter Brueggemann explains that, if you seek a prophet in the world today, you will likely find them in the "subcommunities that stand in tension with the dominant community in any political economy."[4] Like Jesus, prophets most often arise from the undercommons who feel the weight of imperial powers that seek to squelch their hope.

Given their role, the prophet's work is often deconstructive in scope. They are the ones who call out the individuals who perpetrate wrongdoing, exploit the poor, press down the heavy-laden, corrupt people and institutions, divide the church, and accumulate power and wealth for selfish enjoyment. Like the prophets of the Hebrew Bible, today's prophets are also the ones who speak to the people of God bluntly when they have gone astray. Modern prophets speak to the church in love, beckoning her to return to God and away from the treasures of our world. They are vital in seeking the common good in one's community because they are the ones who name all that is decisively *not* good and what requires repair so that something new can be built.

Today, this deconstructive work often looks like Christians who are methodically dismantling their faith brick by brick, testing the integrity and purpose of each part of the whole. It can also look like an explosion (and, perhaps more often, implosion): an abuse scandal rocks a church community to its core, partisan divides begin to pit congregants against one another, a pastor has no theological answer for or response to the injustices of our world. When the safeguards that protect those in power fail and their wrongdoings are exposed, the communities they lead can crumble. When congregations see no viable path to cooperation across lines of difference, churches begin to split. Witnessing this, we might assume that de-

4. Walter Brueggemann, *The Prophetic Imagination*, fortieth anniversary ed. (Fortress, 2018), xxx.

construction cannot be part of building; but that couldn't be further from the truth.

—

As a student in downtown Chicago, I worked for a carpentry team that spent every summer remodeling an old apartment building that the school owned. Soon after the semester ended, we set out our plan of action. On a large whiteboard, we meticulously scheduled contractors, plumbers, carpenters, painters, and cleaning crews to all move through the building without getting in one another's way. Yet, within a week, our plan was in shambles. Crews were stepping on one another's toes, supplies were running out, and new problems were discovered each day. Despite our best efforts, no amount of planning could solve the real problem: the building itself was crumbling from within. We were putting a Band-Aid over an amputated limb. Our plan amounted to installing new headlights on a car with a bad engine. To build something that could last, we first needed to destroy what was currently there.

In the same way, amid its destruction, prophetic work is also constructive. In searching through the rubble, prophets do not only critique. They also bring life and hope to people and communities by offering a vision—a promise—of what awaits us on the horizon of change. "It is precisely the dialectic of criticizing and energizing," says Brueggemann, "that can let us be seriously faithful to God."[5]

A good builder knows how to assess a building and decide if it needs to come down. Communities led by immoral and abusive leaders might send repair crews through to patch leaking pipes and broken fixtures, but the building can only stand for so long. This is why deconstruction is a necessary part of building. Prophets who deconstruct their faith can say, "I lived in this building, and it is no good! It will fall apart; but here is what we can salvage." Good builders also hold on to the end goal. They salvage the usable material

5. Brueggemann, *The Prophetic Imagination*, 4.

and resource new supplies to reconstruct something new without getting lost or trapped by the rubble. They dig their hands into the dirt to determine whether good produce can grow (Matt. 13:24–30). They examine the foundation to see if it is sturdy (Matt. 7:24–27; 1 Cor. 3:9–15). However, prophets cannot do this work on their own. Once a prophetic imagination is offered and the good resources are salvaged, priests and kings must come along to continue the building project.

The Priest and the People of God

I remember the first time I walked into an Anglican church. The entrance was not marked by the large stone arches of a cathedral. Instead, I was greeted by the metal detectors of a public school in the Uptown neighborhood of Chicago. The sanctuary was not adorned with wooden pews or a baptismal font. It was a series of long, descending carpeted stairs that led to a small stage at the bottom where a cross was set up and bread and wine were laid out. Father Aaron—the first religious "Father" I had ever met—greeted me dressed in his green priestly vestments. As someone raised in megachurch evangelicalism where pastors wore bright shirts and skinny jeans, I found it odd to take in. But not long into the service, it all began to make sense. No matter the decor or venue, Fr. Aaron did what any good priest does: He transformed the space into an opportunity to commune with God. He took an ordinary, mundane space and filled it with holy significance. "When we see the world as created and redeemed by God," Fr. Aaron writes in his book *Earth Filled with Heaven*, "we see it sacramentally." "Our world, fallen and broken though it may be, is crammed with the glory of God. Even in the darkest corners, a hidden lamp shines."[6]

Seeing the world sacramentally, "crammed with the glory of

6. Aaron Damiani, *Earth Filled with Heaven: Finding Life in Liturgy, Sacraments, and Other Ancient Practices of the Church* (Moody, 2022), 10.

God," is the good and sacred work of priests. Their task is to create mediums through which humanity might recognize and dwell in God's presence. Just as Christ serves as the mediator between God and creation, those who serve in this earthly role build pathways to commune with God. Some believers recognize this priestly work as a vocation, seek ordination and education, and lead communities of worship across the world. Pastors are tasked with leading the community under their care through the liturgies and rhythms of worship: singing, confession, proclamation, communion, and the like.

However, this ministry also extends beyond those who lead a congregation. As the people of God, commissioned to carry the gospel into the world, we are a priesthood of believers. Come to Christ "like living stones," writes the apostle Peter, and "let yourselves be built into a spiritual house, to be a holy priesthood" (1 Pet. 2:5). He continues, "You are a chosen people, a royal priesthood, a holy nation, God's own people, in order that you may proclaim the excellence of him who called you out of darkness into his marvelous light" (2:9). Where the priest in the Hebrew law functioned as the mediator between the Israelites and God, Peter now proclaims that all believers are tasked with this sacred vocation. No special group solely mediates God's presence to us—*we* are the hands and feet of Christ, bringing about God's good work in the world today.

As a priesthood of believers, we are tasked with being a eucharistic presence in our neighborhoods. In an interview with *Sojourners* magazine, theologian Jonathan Tran reminds us that Christ's priestly statement, "This is my body, given for you," points us to the redemptive possibilities of our world, which are "fundamentally structured towards grace, justice, and mercy."[7] Tran explains that another way to imagine Christ's declaration here is to hear him say, "Here's my body, given to this neighborhood." This shift emphasizes

7. Josiah R. Daniels and Jonathan Tran, "What DEI Trainings and Evangelical Retreats Have in Common," *Sojourners*, January 9, 2024, https://tinyurl.com/ymew47uu.

that the bread we are called to share is not only the loaf found at the communion table. It is also the bread that stocks food pantries, the "bread" that supports congregants in financial need, the "bread" that provides space for grief and lamentation, the "bread" that nourishes a soul craving a sense of belonging and purpose. It is the bread that cultivates the common good. Priests build through the holy work of breaking bread and feeding others.

There is a temptation when invoking this sacramental language to frame this work as discovering the "extraordinary in the ordinary," a common phrase that has graced countless books and sermons. However, it misses a more fundamental, God-given reality: The ordinary *is* sacred. We do not need to search the depths of the "ordinary" to find the sacred. It is already present on the surface—in the loaf of bread and cup of wine, in pigments and hues that grace an artist's canvas, and in the sapling that digs its roots into the dirt and ascends into the sky. In her poem "Backward Miracle," Kay Ryan speaks of a "sacramental refusal to multiply, reclaiming the single loaf and the single fish thereby."[8] Rather than getting caught up in the project of making meaning, Ryan reminds us of the miracle of simply being, which comes before any attempt to make meaning.[9] The priest's task is to make these sacred things known.

To continue this analogy of the building, priests function as the architects. If prophets salvage and resource the material, priests take inventory of what is gathered and sketch out how this new home will be laid out. Stewards of God's presence in the world, priests provide a blueprint of a space that will bring those who enter closer to God. They sketch out a food pantry with a kitchen that can feed the community and a dining space that can seat everyone. They

8. Kay Ryan, "Backward Miracle," quoted in Christian Wiman, *Zero at the Bone: Fifty Entries Against Despair* (Farrar, Straus & Giroux, 2023), 180.

9. Christian Wiman, offering his own commentary on Ryan's poem, explains how "the miraculous is so 'common' (as in beneath us) that sometimes we need to be jolted back by and to the particular. Don't be too quick to transcend, her poem tells us. Being precedes meaning." *Zero at the Bone*, 181.

outline the plans for a community farm that will produce bounties of fruits and vegetables without exhausting the soil. Priests work toward the common good by drawing the communities closer to both God and neighbor.

The King and the Political Realm

Kings are deeply embedded in our political life. While this includes those who might hold government office, this role extends well beyond city hall. Political life, in this sense, is more than a competing two-party system. Politics involves how our common life is formed, normed, and sustained.[10] It contains, as Rubem Alves poetically describes, "people, imagination in flight, hands joined, building friendly places, habitations, paradises, where there should be no unnecessary meaning nor provoked tears, because the compatibility of human beings with nature accompanies the compatibility between human beings."[11]

The task of a king is to govern, support, and promote some kind of meaningful, common life that recognizes our different—often competing and conflicting—visions of the good. Alongside prophets and priests, kings can meaningfully respond to the crises and challenges of our local community and country by governing big institutions, funding other builders, and stewarding systems that promote shared flourishing.

This is what our political systems are supposed to do well. The liturgies of our politics should help give voice, representation, and decision-making power to all people and communities. At their best, political practices like town halls, canvassing, holding local office, voting—and also protesting, striking, and organizing—have

10. Luke Bretherton, *Christ and the Common Life: Political Theology and the Case for Democracy* (Eerdmans, 2019), 2.

11. Rubem A. Alves, *I Believe in the Resurrection of the Body* (Wipf & Stock, 1986), 47.

accomplished incredible things in our nation.[12] In recent memory, we can think of the student encampments organized across America in the spring of 2024 to protest America's active military funding to support the genocide in Gaza and the subsequent profit of businesses, institutions, and organizations from this violence. The stimulus checks offered during the COVID-19 pandemic were also an exercise of kingly power that helped families and businesses survive a global crisis. Looking back, we can also think of the civil rights movement, which fundamentally reshaped the landscape of America through new voting and immigration legislation. This movement was modeled after organizers like Ida B. Wells and other diligent coalition builders who brought together people across lines of difference to protest mass lynchings in America. We emulate Christ's role as king when we pursue the good of the public through the stewardship of relationships, resources, and power, no matter the scale. Kings use whatever agency they possess to seek the good of their community.

Bestowed with great power, those functioning in a kingly role must be all the more diligent to avoid the temptations that power brings. It is no secret that our political system is fraught with leaders who align themselves with people and policies that give them power over their neighbor rather than legislation and rights that empower

12. I appreciate how Oliver O'Donovan puts it: "Earthly events of liberation, rule and community-foundation provide us with partial indications of what God is doing in human history; while correspondingly, we must look to the horizon of God's redemptive purposes if we are to grasp the full meaning of political events that pass before our eyes . . . politics may, and indeed does, serve as a source of religious imagery, part of that broken glass whose reflections the soul transcends as it moves on and up towards the divine glory." *The Desire of the Nations: Rediscovering the Roots of Political Theology* (Cambridge University Press, 1996), 2. See also Eric Gregory, "The Boldness of Analogy: Civic Virtues and Augustinian Eudaimonism," in *The Authority of the Gospel: Explorations in Moral and Political Theology in Honor of Oliver O'Donovan*, ed. Robert Song and Brent Waters (Eerdmans, 2015).

their neighbor. Kings in our world today must not be idealistic about such things. They must acknowledge that democracy is not off the hook for the power hierarchy it prioritizes and the undercommons—the marginalized and silenced communities—it creates. Our political and democratic systems are fallible and worthy of critique.

In this moment of American democracy where leaders are placing a crown on their head, those serving in a kingly role must remember that Christ, who held the greatest power, refused to place his kingship under the empire's reign.[13] In other words, if following Christ in this kingly work leads to self-glorification and excessive adornment, something has gone horribly awry. The kingly work of Christ is always for others—particularly those on the margins of society.[14]

Kings act out of a shared commitment to human flourishing. Their task is, as Luke Bretherton writes, to foster "faithful, hopeful, and loving ways of being alive *with* and *for* others."[15] If we do not have a vested interest in the good of our neighbors, then we will never cultivate a common life. If we fail to develop this common life, our politics will only be a vehicle for pursuing our self-interest and personal comfort. But when a common life is cultivated, we don't need to leave our social or theological beliefs at the door. Instead, we come together across lines of difference where we ultimately end up better understanding ourselves because we can contrast the hues of our beliefs against those of our neighbor.

The task of the king is ultimately to help shape our political life and

13. For more on how to do this well, see Joash P. Thomas, *The Justice of Jesus: Reimagining Your Church's Life Together to Pursue Liberation and Wholeness* (Brazos, 2025).

14. This follows the tradition of Catholic social teaching, which holds firmly to the belief that God holds a "preferential option for the poor." See Gustavo Gutiérrez, *A Theology of Liberation* (Orbis Books, 1988). Also Pope Francis's encyclical *Fratelli Tutti (On Fraternity and Social Friendship)*.

15. Bretherton, *Christ and the Common Life*, 2.

action toward a greater purpose than politics itself.[16] Kings use their power—both given and accumulated— to love our neighbors and seek their good by cultivating communities built on equity, dignity, and belonging. When we do this well, politics becomes a way of attending to the needs of others. No matter where this kingly work takes place, the task remains the same: to seek the good of the public.

Buildings and Builders

At this point, you may be wondering *who* is tasked with the actual work of building. In this illustration, who is the one picking up the hammer to assemble the framework for the house or the garden shovel to begin breaking into the soil? The answer is *all of us.* We all have a part to play in building toward a common good.

All Christians are tasked with building because we worship a God who builds, creates, and sustains. God's creative work is how we are first introduced to God in Genesis 1. God speaks into the void of the cosmos, creating light and life. At the beginning of the world, God builds. Before anything else, this is what the Scriptures desire for us to know. But God's building work does not stop there. It continues today. The psalmist reminds us,

> Unless the Lord builds the house,
> those who build it labor in vain. (Ps. 127:1)

God's people are tasked with following their creator in this building work. God commands the Israelites to build the ark of the covenant and a tabernacle so that God might dwell with them (Exod. 25–27;

16. Michael Wear puts it well: We must understand that the crisis today is not that Christians are now politically homeless, but rather that they ever thought they could make their home in politics at all. *The Spirit of Our Politics: Spiritual Formation and the Renovation of Public Life* (Zondervan, 2024), xv.

36:1) and to build altars where God has provided so that they might remember that God has blessed them (Exod. 20:22–24). When Israel is exiled to Babylon, God's command to build remains as the prophet Jeremiah instructs them to build homes, plant gardens, sink familial roots, and seek the welfare of the city (Jer. 29:4–9).

Jesus, too, uses stories and illustrations of building to describe his kingdom work. He tells Peter that he is the rock upon which Jesus will build his church (Matt. 16:18), likens faithful obedience to God to a house that is built with a firm foundation (Luke 6:46–49), and reminds his disciples that he is preparing a place for them in his Father's house (John 14:1–3). The New Testament writers also refer to Christ's disciples as God's building (1 Cor. 3:9). In Ephesians, Paul writes that those who are in Christ are "built together spiritually into a dwelling place for God" (2:19–22). In 1 Corinthians, Paul calls Christ followers "God's coworkers" and likens himself to a "wise master builder" (3:9–11).

As Christians, our construction work is rooted in a desire to worship God with our hearts and our labor. As Paul writes to the Colossians, "Whatever task you must do, work as if your soul depends on it, as for the Lord and not for humans" (3:23). Therefore, *what* we build and *how* we build it should not be motivated by profit or scale. Instead, following in God's call to goodness, we build to give away. This does not mean it is wrong to have a successful business that flourishes financially or a congregation that grows in size. However, what matters is how we order our loves and values as builders. If profit or expansion is the highest goal, then builders will likely be quick to cut corners, raise rent, and underpay workers. But, if the goal is human flourishing and public health, builders can focus on growing deeper with their congregation or offering a quality product rather than adding more chairs to the sanctuary or building the most extensive client base. We must remember what God has given to *use*—power, equity, wealth, resources—and what God intends for us to *enjoy*: God and neighbor.

—

In their powerful book on community organizing, Kelly Hayes and Mariame Kaba rightly conclude that "transformative change happens when we are willing to build the things that we know must exist."[17] This is why, as we gather around the communal table, we will soon find that we are not alone in this faith-driven building work. A Jewish gardener may start an urban farm because they see how the Hebrew Scriptures are filled with a mandate to care for creation and serve those in need. A Muslim immigrant may build a chai shop for their community to taste authentic drinks and cuisine from another part of the world. A Sikh community may build a *gurdwara* to provide a central place for worship and feed their community through the daily practice of *langar*—a free community meal. A Hindu therapist may build a community health center that offers free meditation and yoga classes to their community. People of faith build what we know *must* exist for the flourishing of our neighbors.

What Christians can offer to this collective task of building is "a hopeful architecture" that "communicates that people and places are worthy of care and respect." As Norman Wirzba explains, "By reflecting a loving intention in their design and construction, neighborhoods and buildings convey that the people who work and play and rest there are also loved."[18] Following in this hopeful architecture, Christians who build emulate a God who creates to share with others. Like goodness, our disposition toward creation must be nonpossessive. Just as God creates to bestow, we also must build—homes, gardens, institutions, playgrounds, and community centers—to share them with others.

17. Kelly Hayes and Mariame Kaba, *Let This Radicalize You: Organizing and the Revolution of Reciprocal Care* (Haymarket Books, 2023), 12.

18. Norman Wirzba, *Love's Braided Dance: Hope in a Time of Crisis* (Yale University Press, 2024), 125.

Faithful Presence

One question remains: *What* will we build? The answer to that question will depend on where we are located. There is no single design or city plan to copy and paste from place to place. Every neighborhood has its own needs. As builders and companions, it is our job to survey and intimately understand the landscape we are working with and then meet the needs of that community.

To do this, we must take up the practice of faithful presence.[19] Following the example of God's action in the world, faithful presence looks like emulating God's incarnate work in the world, which is marked by goodness, love, and community. To build the kingdom of God, Jesus does not remain aloof. God enters into creation to be near it, to share in this common life, and to cultivate a shared desire for the things of God. Jesus chooses to be faithfully present in and with creation.[20]

To build spaces of belonging, we must understand that faithful presence is required for belonging and community to blossom. We must attend to the lived experience of those who share our community. We must listen to our neighbors, learn the history of where we dwell, understand its needs and vulnerabilities, and then work with others already present to build something worthwhile and good. As the philosopher James Davison Hunter concludes, faithful presence "is a quality of commitment that is active, not passive; intentional, not accidental; covenantal, not contractual."[21]

In my experience organizing and working within various institutions, building rooted in faithful presence is always marked by a vi-

19. While this term is expansive, I first encountered it in the work of James Davison Hunter. See *To Change the World: The Irony, Tragedy, & Possibility of Christianity in the Late Modern World* (Oxford University Press, 2010).

20. Rubem Alves puts it simply: "What the doctrine of the incarnation whispers to us is that God, eternally, wants a body like ours." *I Believe*, 7–8.

21. Hunter, *To Change the World*, 240–43.

sion of belonging.[22] Building—and cultivating—belonging is an art and skill that requires study and practice. Creating this kind of community doesn't often happen spontaneously. It requires thoughtfulness and intentionality. To build toward belonging requires considering the lived experience of those we are building for.

Faithful presence is a eucharistic presence. We join God in the neighborhood, sharing the bread of Christ's body broken for us. Like the psalmist, we beckon our neighbors to t*aste and see that the Lord is good*. This communion, though, is also shown through the way we attend to and accompany our neighbors. "If there is a possibility for human flourishing in a world such as ours," Hunter concludes, "it begins when God's word of love becomes flesh in us, is embodied in us, is enacted through us and in doing so, a trust is forged between the word spoken and the reality to which it speaks; to the words we speak and the realities to which we, the church, point."[23]

The task of building spaces of belonging rooted in faithful presence points us to what is most important: the sustained and flourishing life of the community, the neighborhood, and the people contained in them. As prophets, priests, and kings, we are bestowed with a creative, God-given command to build good things that can be shared. In doing so, we cultivate a common good for our community marked by participation and inclusion. When we build toward belonging, we proclaim hope in a healthy commons that seeks the good of the whole.

22. For more on this, see my chapter "A Lived Theology of Belonging," in A*wake, Emerging, and Connected Meditations on Justice from a Missing Generation*, ed. Victoria Turner (SCM Press, 2024).

23. Hunter, *To Change the World*, 241.

5

WE LIVE AS NEIGHBORS

"As they carried on along and met more people Furlong did and did not know, he found himself asking was there any point in being alive without helping one another. Was it possible to carry on along through all the years, the decades, through an entire life, without once being brave enough to go against what was there and yet call yourself a Christian, and face yourself in the mirror?"

—Claire Keegan, *Small Things like These*

"What is hope? It is the pre-sentiment that imagination is more real and reality is less real that it looks."

—Rubem A. Alves,
Tomorrow's Child: Imagination, Creativity, and the Rebirth of Culture

Can you imagine it now? Can you picture a world where we live as neighbors? Can you see the table and all who are present there? I hope that, as you've read this short book, this vision has come into view like shades of light and color breaking through Polaroid film.

We live as those who are formed by and toward God's presence at the table. We live into God's calling to love others radically, seek goodness in our world, and cultivate communities of belonging. We live as neighbors through practices of compassion and humility, lament and resonance, translation and accompaniment. We live as builders who follow Christ's prophetic, priestly, and royal offices.

One piece, though, is still missing. It is the glue that holds this good work and our place in it together. It is the vision of shared flourishing that keeps us on track. It is the hope that keeps our ship steady in troubled waters. We must seek a common good with a resurrected imagination.

Resurrected Imagination

Resurrected imagination changes how we love our neighbors by attuning us to the cycles of death and resurrection in our world. It is a vision of our common life seen through the kaleidoscope of Christ's resurrection, which shifts how we perceive reality and the possibilities of our world. The resurrected Christ reminds us that if we live our lives constantly glancing up at the sky awaiting his return, we will miss the active work of the Holy Spirit in the world today. A resurrected imagination doesn't focus on what is beyond this world. It is concerned with the good and redemptive possibilities within it.

This is more than wishful thinking. It is a vision of possibility—of the world as it might be—that changes how we form community and engage with the world around us. Resurrected imagination, in this creative sense, is like a child who transforms his backyard into a kingdom where sticks become swords, a trampoline turns into a lava pit, and footballs are launched across the yard like heavy artillery. Even as children, we know that the good and creative possibilities contained in our imagination are always beckoning to be brought into the world and turned into new realities.[1] A resurrected imagination is not cultivated by retreating from the world but through being charged and chastened by our encounter with the world and the lives of others.[2]

When we live attuned to the reality of resurrection, even death cannot stomp out the embers of hope. Truly, a resurrected imagination makes us a people of deep, unwavering hope even in a world that is not right. Living in the light of the resurrection instills in us a confident hope that redemption is near and that the potential for change remains at our fingertips—that we exist not in a long winter but in a prolonged spring that awaits the flower's first bloom. A resurrected imagination invites us to, like children, dream of a world marked by love and goodness and find creative and innovative solutions to achieve that vision. *I believe in the resurrection of the body and the life everlasting.*

1. Paul Ricoeur speaks of the imagination as the mind's power to produce new realities. See *Lectures on Imagination* (University of Chicago Press, 2024).

2. Christian Wiman writes, "These days I am impatient with poetry that is not steeped in, marred and transfigured by, the world. By that I don't necessarily mean poetry that has some obvious social concern or is meticulous with its descriptions, but a poetry in which you can feel that the imagination of the poet has been both charged and chastened by a full encounter with the world and other lives." *My Bright Abyss: Meditations of a Modern Believer* (Farrar, Straus & Giroux, 2013), 46.

This resurrected imagination does not unlock the mysteries of the universe or the answer to the problem of evil. Neither does it give us the eyes to see everything happening in the world at once. Instead, this new perception cultivates in us an attention to the intimate—to the infinities that abound in our world, not beyond it. To possess—or be possessed *by*—a resurrected imagination is to see the physical world around us and perceive the sacred and spiritual significance present within it. While this may sound like a daunting task, we can begin cultivating a resurrected imagination by bending down and touching the soil beneath our feet.

Hopeful Gardeners

"How does the garden appear?" asks Rubem Alves. His answer is poetic and powerful:

> First of all, there must be a gardener. There must be a desire. The imagination must soar. There is the hard, dry land, thorns, the sun that punishes the cracked soil, the springs that don't exist. . . . People come, look, their eyes suffer. Because they do not see just with their eyes. They see with the soul, desire. Everything could be different. And they dream. Imagination soars. The garden, fountains, shade, flowers, breeze, the locust chattering in the afternoons and the birds in the mornings; nights are friendly because the fences keep the wild animals away; feet can run unshod because there are no thorns; and bodies are uncovered to the caress of the breeze and the play of the fountains. Imagination calls to the body, mobilizes the hands, and work comes, which transforms suffering into smiles, deserts into gardens, deserted places into pleasant living spaces. Home, friendly city. City, nothing more than a garden for a lot of people.[3]

3. Rubem A. Alves, *I Believe in the Resurrection of the Body* (Wipf & Stock, 1986), 46.

Gardens begin with a resurrected imagination.

This should not come as a surprise. Gardeners are well acquainted with the patterns of life and death. They prune leaves from plants and pick fresh fruit from the vine. They bend back old crops to make way for new ones. Amid death and decay, gardeners can see and name the abundant patterns of transformation present in the natural cycles of life and death that God has put in place all around us. As my friend Lauren Daniels Judge, a theologian and ecologist, reminds me, "We do not need to invent these patterns or cycles. They are something that we need to come in relationship with through a posture of learning to see that these patterns are already in play."[4]

Think of a compost pile.[5] Taking what we often consider "waste," we fill compost piles with an abundance of organic life that deconstructs brown and green material down to its most basic forms: carbon and nitrogen. Spiraling toward decay, death is not the final word of the compost pile. Instead, old coffee grounds, eggshells, rotten fruit, vegetable scraps, grass clippings, and fallen leaves are confronted with worms, sowbugs, nematodes, and microorganisms that work together to transform these materials into an accessible, new life that can enliven tired soil. As liberation theologian Yanan Melo writes, "The powers of life and death, decay and resurrection, are occurring all around us in the deep dark of the earth to sustain all that lives and resurrect dead matter back to life."[6]

4. I am incredibly grateful for Lauren's work as a farmer, scholar, and educator, which illuminates the many ways that gardens exemplify a resurrected imagination. I have learned much from her and her work at Plant Relationships, a small business cultivating a sustainable, interconnected network of gardens that serve as vibrant hubs for learning, sharing, and cultivating a deeper connection to the food we eat and the land we inhabit. Learn more about her work at https://www.plantrelationships.com.

5. Jeff Chu offers a beautiful meditation on compost in *Good Soil: The Education of an Accidental Farmhand* (Convergent Books, 2025).

6. Yanan Melo, "Black Body and Blood: The Eucharistic Imagination of

To be sure, there are easier ways to amend malnourished soil. For example, chemical pellets can be purchased and introduced to the garden bed. But farmers who possess a resurrected imagination can see this substitute for what it is: synthetic. Pellets do not contain true, biological life. They are a quick fix. Organic nourishment can only be achieved through the toil and intentionality of the compost pile.

If our communities today are like soil in need of nourishment, then our task is to possess a resurrected imagination that can see the microscopic life of the compost pile. We are not satisfied with synthetic substitutes; we work to produce the fruit of the spirit that is abundant with organic life. To do this work, gardeners—and Christians—must see through death and decomposition to the resurrected life beyond it.

This does not dismiss or negate the painful reality before them: a harvest ravaged by animals, budding flowers trampled underfoot, the dry heat of a drought drawing the life out of once vibrant and full vines. Yet, those who possess a resurrected imagination know that this death does not work *against* life; it works *toward* new life. Resurrection is microorganisms digesting material to transform it into renewing fertilizer. It is the prophet denouncing systems of exploitation and injustice so priests and kings can start to salvage materials and rebuild. It is Jesus sacrificing himself for us so we may experience life in abundance. *Everything could be different. Imagination soars.*

Both the gardener and the resurrected Christ remind us that death is both a part of life and necessary to create new life. The messiness and grief that accompany loss remind us that we are still alive. This doesn't make the reality of death any easier.[7] But it does

---

Racial Capitalism (and How the Earth Groans in Defiance)" (presented at the Afterlives of Slavery Conference in Washington, DC, October 19, 2023). Paper shared through private correspondence.

7. Take, for example, the tears that flow from Jesus's eyes as he stands

give a reason for hope. Just as there can be no comfort without first weeping (Matt. 5:4), without death, there can be no resurrection.

—

Norman Wirzba explains that when we possess radical, resurrected hope, "grief and lament are not forms of resignation in the face of this world's pain and violation. They are, instead, forms of power that fuel a person's commitment to 'join with all the living' and offer a healing hand of help." He continues, "Hope is a way of being in which people commit themselves to the healing of our wounded world and, in so doing, communicate a future that is worth striving for. It is an orientation and a disposition that is animated by the power of love that affirms the sanctity of this life and this world."[8]

Aimee Byrd says this another way: Hope, like the resurrected Christ, *bears* scars.[9] Resurrected life is never completely detached from the death that precedes it. Jesus does not return to the world as something new or immaterial. He is the same divine God-man who walked with his disciples, proclaiming the good news of salvation to those who believe. The Jesus that Mary mistakes for a gardener (which, in a cosmic sense, he is!) outside and beyond the tomb is the same Jesus who wept at the death of his friend, who healed the sick, who grew tired, and who ate with those who lived at the margins of society. Jesus returns in the same scarred flesh.

Jesus and the gardener remind us of the possibility of change amid the world's despair. Down to the unobservable workings of the earth's soil, God has written a story of new life into our world. The

---

beside a lifeless Lazarus. Jesus *knows* what will happen. He will bring life back into Lazarus's body. Jesus's knowledge of resurrection does not spare him the intense feeling of grief.

8. Norman Wirzba, *Love's Braided Dance: Hope in a Time of Crisis* (Yale University Press, 2024), 13–14.

9. Aimee Byrd, *The Hope in Our Scars: Finding the Bride of Christ in the Underground of Disillusionment* (Brazos, 2024), 15. See also Shelly Rambo, *Resurrecting Wounds: Living in the Afterlife of Trauma* (Baylor University Press, 2017).

creative possibilities of a resurrected imagination ultimately lead us to a profound hope that the soil of our communities is fertile and ready for the seeds of change. When we dig our hands into the soil of our gardens to plant goodness, beauty, and truth, we attune ourselves to the resurrection work already taking place. "Faith is not faith in some state beyond change. Faith is faith in change," says Christian Wiman. There is great joy "in the deep, implicit peace whose surest promise of reality is the miraculous capacity we have—in a work of art, a gesture of love, or any of the other ways in which we acknowledge the God who is this ever-perfecting process—to imagine it."[10]

Fragments

The hope of a resurrected imagination orients us toward our neighbors. Rather than philosophizing and speaking in circles about infinite and unknowable things, this sacred perception draws us to God's good action in the neighborhood. When we join with people in this hopeful way, we will soon find that we hold only fragments of a larger story: We see but in glimpses, taste but in bites, smell but in wafts, and hear but in echoes reverberating through space far greater than we can know. A resurrected imagination requires us to pick up these fragments we hold loosely and make sense of them by bringing them into a larger community. Together, we are guided by the Holy Spirit as we come to the table and piece together our experiences, traditions, histories, fears, and loves to reveal God's overarching story of redemption, drawing the world to himself. Truly, fragmentation longs for integration. The desire of our story is to become whole.

Fragments, of course, leave open the gray, in-between space of finitude. These materials do not perfectly match. But this is where the hard work of the organic, living, compost-nourished love con-

10. Wiman, *My Bright Abyss*, 104.

tinues. It is like the Japanese art of *kintsugi*, where broken pottery is mended to create something new and beautiful.[11] This art form takes fractured pieces of clay and binds them together with glowing strands of metallic dust mixed into an adhesive lacquer. Holding a piece of *kintsugi* in your hand, you can trace with your finger where the gold dust widens and thins, matching the fragmented clay. It is fractured dissonance returned to a resurrected resonance.

If we could hold our communities in the same way, we would find something similar. When our stories, traditions, and liturgies align, the practices of gathering and belonging serve as a thin adhesive. However, when there are large gaps and cracks between unaligned fragments, we must mend them with heavy lines of love, humility, generosity, and justice. It is this interwoven play of thin and heavy lines that makes *kintsugi* so compelling. Each piece carries with it a history of destruction and repair, of fracture becoming whole again. It doesn't hide brokenness; it transforms its past into a lasting beauty. *Kintsugi* hope bears scars.

The gardener and *kintsugi* artist have a resurrected imagination that can see the beautiful repair amid the fractures of broken clay and the microcosmic workings of the garden. Where others see break and decay, they see wholeness and transformation. This lasting repair—this resurrected life—does not happen overnight. It is accomplished through long labor, intentionality, and investment. The same is true of our communities. Cultivating this common life requires us to step outside and dig our hands into the soil. We must come to the table and, with our neighbors, hold the gathered fragments in our hands to feel and experience them. We must join in loving community amid our brokenness and division with a resurrected imagination that can proclaim the hope of transformed life beyond our present moment.

11. Aimee Byrd offers her own theological analysis of *kintsugi* in *The Hope in Our Scars*, 201–3. See also Makoto Fujimura, *Art and Faith: A Theology of Making* (Yale University Press, 2021).

Becoming Neighbors

I believe that the good life we all seek is found in loving and enjoying God and neighbor. It is, in Augustine's words, the life that exists in "completely harmonious fellowship in the enjoyment of God, and each other in God."[12] To deeply love our neighbors is our highest calling because this love flows through our relationship with God out into the world to both friend and enemy, neighbor and stranger.

When we live with a resurrected imagination, we begin to live for the sake of others rather than for our own gain. We are drawn to the table because God and our neighbor are there. We give of ourselves for the good of the whole because this sacred perception acknowledges that my flourishing is intimately bound to my neighbor's flourishing.

The transformative work of neighbor love shifts our desire from "controlling" a chaotic world to "living as neighbors" in a world we can't control.[13] Recognizing Christ's lordship frees us to move in and through the world in the pursuit of this divine love and goodness present all around us. It compels us to follow in the way of Jesus, who calls us to take up our cross, not a sword. Loving our neighbors transforms our minds and hearts precisely because it makes us aware of the extent of God's divine love for us. When we love rightly through a resurrected imagination, we are freed to participate in God's good, loving, and redemptive work happening all around us.

Whether you have skimmed over the pages of this book or read

12. Augustine, *The City of God Against the Pagans*, trans. Henry Bettenson (Penguin Books, 2004), 19.17. See also Miroslav Volf, Matthew Croasmun, and Ryan McAnnally-Linz, *Life Worth Living: A Guide to What Matters Most* (Open Field, 2023).

13. This framing of living as neighbors "in a world we can't control" is indebted to John Inazu and Megan Johnson, who began the Evangelicals in a Diverse Democracy project at Interfaith America, which I had the privilege of taking up in my time on staff there.

them word for word, I hope this has become abundantly true: faith that is formed by love for our neighbors leads us to a shared vision of a common good. Our calling is to be the kind of people who set tables, who provide for those in need, who love unconditionally, who build good and beautiful things, who proclaim the blessedness of the undercommons, and who seek the flourishing of the whole.

How will we live? *We live as neighbors.*

—

"*What do you think? Which of the three became a neighbor to the man attacked by robbers?*"

"The one who treated him kindly," the religion scholar responded.

Jesus said, "*Go and do the same*" (Luke 10:36–37 *The Message*).

ACKNOWLEDGMENTS

This book is the result of many people I've bumped against in this world and the places I've met them. I am grateful for the many neighbors who've shaped these words as we've shared in this common life.

Annah Kuriakose, Yanan Melo, and Ryan Snyder read the first drafts of these chapters, providing encouragement, feedback, and insight. Annah, in particular, exemplified Paul Farmer's faithful practice of accompaniment in the countless hours spent sitting with me in the nebulas—the amorphous space dust—of big questions and ideas. Mark Fraley, Chelsea Langston Bombino, Lauren Daniels Judge, David Chao, and Josiah R. Daniels offered their time and expertise in abundance. My colleagues and friends from Interfaith America—Joey Haynes, Rollie Olson, Suzanne Watts Henderson, Megan Johnson, Anne Coyne, Silma Suba, Katherine O'Brien, Sara Rahim, Allie Vroegop, Harmeet Kamboj, Becca Hartman-Pickrell, Mary Ellen Giess, John Inazu, and Eboo Patel—let me derail our meetings with the musings that overflowed from my writing sessions. Interfaith America's Emerging Leaders Network also consistently made space for me during retreats, convenings, and meetings to workshop ideas. Suraj Arshanapally, Chris RayAlexander, Anu Gorukanti, Tahil Sharma, Anastasia Young, Matt Segil, Kenji Kuramitsu, David Katibah, Sabina Pappu, Rafia Khader, Nikhil Mandalaparthy, and many others modeled this vision of this book as we've gathered around many tables over the years.

The seeds of this book were planted in Princeton. Conversations with John Walker, Sean Pomory, Pat Kiernan, Derek Wu, Jalen Baker, Aidan Meyer, J. D. Tyler and many others between Nassau Street and Loetscher Place are woven throughout its pages. Its roots are dug into endless rows of books in Wright Library, the pews of the University Chapel, and the sun-warmed tables around the Gingered Peach. A few miles up Highway 27, Jacob's Well in North Brunswick modeled this vision of the common good cultivated at a shared table that remained at the front of my mind as I wrote this book.

Augsburg University's Riverside Innovation Hub offered a community of young writers and experienced leaders who helped me place neighbor love on the ground. Jeremy Meyers, Kristina Frugé, Nicholas Tangen, Baird Linke, Kayla Zopfi, Kristen Glass Perez, and Soong-Chan Rah all spoke words of life into this book. The Good Road Network, a learning laboratory of Christian leaders I started in 2022, became a space to work through questions and ideas with thoughtful and engaged Christian leaders working on the ground, living out this vision and seeking the common good through love of neighbor. Princeton Seminary's Polaris Network spoke into the early months of writing, reaffirming the truth that faith is always being formed. The Kairos Collective in Milwaukee helped ground this book in a living, worshiping community. Last, Zach Wilt, Daniel Cameron, Nate Brumbaugh, and Ben Sanford became a community of laughter and belonging that kept my mind fresh and spirits high after long days of writing.

This book's existence is especially indebted to several people. Dr. Ashish Varma opened his door and, to the score of Hans Zimmer's *Batman vs. Superman* soundtrack and Nora Jones's deep cuts, taught me what it means to live faithfully in this world as an Indian American who straddles Delhi and the Midwest, Christmas and Diwali, wheaty beer and a cup of warm chai. Dr. Heath Carter took a bright-eyed seminarian under his wing and instilled in me the confidence to do anything. Pastor Scott Jones shared his pulpit with me as a seminary intern and told me I was a writer. Lisa Ann Cockrel generously gave me the opportunity to live out this statement and, along with Kim Benedict and the team at Eerdmans, helped craft this book into its best form. This is a dream come true. I am forever grateful.

Last, I am thankful for my wife, Emīlija, who has championed me through both success and failure. The path to this book was long and winding. You have been there patiently and faithfully every step of the way.

WORKS CITED

Abhishiktananda, Swami. *Prayer.* New edition. Canterbury Press, 2006.

Allen, Danielle. *Talking to Strangers: Anxieties of Citizenship Since Brown v. Board of Education*. University of Chicago Press, 2004.

Alves, Rubem A. *I Believe in the Resurrection of the Body*. Wipf & Stock, 1986.

———. *Tomorrow's Child: Imagination, Creativity, and the Rebirth of Culture*. Wipf & Stock, 2011.

Auden, W. H. "The Garrison." In *Epistle to a Godson, and Other Poems*. Random House, 1972.

Augustine. *The City of God Against the Pagans*. Translated by Henry Bettenson. Penguin Books, 2004.

———. *Sermons: III/8 (273–305A) on the Saints.* The Works of Saint Augustine: A Translation for the 21st Century. Translated by Edmund Hill. Edited by John E. Rotelle. New City Press, 1994.

Barth, Karl. *God Here and Now*. Translated by Paul M. van Buren. Routledge, 2003.

Battle, Michael. *Desmond Tutu: A Spiritual Biography of South Africa's Confessor*. Westminster John Knox, 2021.

Berry, Wendell. "How to Be a Poet (to Remind Myself)." In *Poetry*, January 2001.

Block, Jennie Weiss. *Paul Farmer: Servant to the Poor*. Liturgical Press, 2018.

Blomberg, Craig L. *Contagious Holiness: Jesus' Meals with Sinners*. New Studies in Biblical Theology. InterVarsity Press, 2005.

Bretherton, Luke. *Christ and the Common Life: Political Theology and the Case for Democracy*. Eerdmans, 2019.

Brueggemann, Walter. *The Prophetic Imagination*. Fortieth anniversary ed. Fortress, 2018.

Byrd, Aimee. *The Hope in Our Scars: Finding the Bride of Christ in the Underground of Disillusionment*. Brazos, 2024.

Chu, Jeff. *Good Soil: The Education of an Accidental Farmhand*. Convergent Books, 2025.

Copeland, M. Shawn. *Enfleshing Freedom: Body, Race, and Being*. Fortress, 2009.

Croasmun, Matthew, and Miroslav Volf. *The Hunger for Home: Food and Meals in the Gospel of Luke*. Baylor University Press, 2022.

Damiani, Aaron. *Earth Filled with Heaven: Finding Life in Liturgy, Sacraments, and Other Ancient Practices of the Church*. Moody, 2022.

Daniels, Josiah R., and Jonathan Tran. "What DEI Trainings and Evangelical Retreats Have in Common." *Sojourners*, January 9, 2024. https://tinyurl.com/ymew47uu.

Day, Keri. *Notes of a Native Daughter: Testifying in Theological Education*. Eerdmans, 2021.

Dean, Kenda Creasy. *Innovating for Love: Joining God's Expedition Through Christian Social Innovation*. Market Square Publishing, 2022.

DeCort, Andrew. *Blessed Are the Others: Jesus' Way in a Violent World*. BitterSweet Books, 2024.

Detrow, Scott, Gabriel J. Sánchez, and Sarah Handel. "He Was a Top Church Official Who Criticized Trump. He Says Christianity Is in Crisis." NPR, August 8, 2023. https://tinyurl.com/4kjm6e5v.

Douglass, Katherine M. *Creative in the Image of God: An Aesthetic Practical Theology of Young Adult Faith*. Cascade, 2020.

Draper, Andrew T. *A Theology of Race and Place: Liberation and Reconciliation in the Works of Jennings and Carter*. Pickwick, 2016.

Farmer, Paul. *To Repair the World: Paul Farmer Speaks to the Next Generation*. Edited by Jonathan L. Weigel. University of California Press, 2013.

Farmer, Paul, and Gustavo Gutiérrez. *In the Company of the Poor: Conver-*

sations with Dr. Paul Farmer and Fr. Gustavo Gutiérrez, edited by Michael Griffin and Jennie Weiss Block. Orbis Books, 2013.

Francis. *Fratelli Tutti*. October 3, 2020. https://tinyurl.com/k2wrp5hd.

Fujimura, Makoto. *Art and Faith: A Theology of Making*. Yale University Press, 2021.

Gregory, Eric. "The Boldness of Analogy: Civic Virtues and Augustinian Eudaimonism." In *The Authority of the Gospel: Explorations in Moral and Political Theology in Honor of Oliver O'Donovan*, edited by Robert Song and Brent Waters. Eerdmans, 2015.

———. *Politics and the Order of Love: An Augustinian Ethic of Democratic Citizenship*. University of Chicago Press, 2008.

Gutiérrez, Gustavo. *A Theology of Liberation*. Orbis Books, 1988.

Harney, Stefano, and Fred Moten. *The Undercommons: Fugitive Planning and Black Study*. Minor Compositions, 2013.

Hayes, Kelly, and Mariame Kaba. *Let This Radicalize You: Organizing and the Revolution of Reciprocal Care*. Haymarket Books, 2023.

Hector, Kevin W. *Christianity as a Way of Life: A Systematic Theology*. Yale University Press, 2023.

Heidegger, Martin. *Being and Time*. Translated by John Macquarrie and Edward Robinson. Harper Perennial Modern Classics, 2008.

Herdt, Jennifer. "Empathy Beyond the In-Group: Stoic Universalism and Augustinian Neighbor-Love." In *Philosophy, Theology and the Sciences* 2, no. 1 (2015): 63–88.

Hicks-Keeton, Jill. *Good Book: How White Evangelicals Save the Bible to Save Themselves*. Fortress, 2023.

Hunter, James Davison. *To Change the World: The Irony, Tragedy, & Possibility of Christianity in the Late Modern World*. Oxford University Press, 2010.

Jennings, Willie James. *Acts: A Theological Commentary on the Bible*. Westminster John Knox, 2017.

———. *After Whiteness: An Education in Belonging*. Eerdmans, 2020.

Kaemingk, Matthew. *Christian Hospitality and Muslim Immigration in an Age of Fear*. Eerdmans, 2018.

Karris, Robert J. *Eating Your Way Through Luke's Gospel*. Liturgical Press, 2006.

Keegan, Claire. *Small Things like These*. Grove, 2021.

Kierkegaard, Søren. *Provocations: Spiritual Writings of Kierkegaard*. Compiled and edited by Charles E. Moore. Orbis Books, 2003.

———. *Sickness unto Death: A Christian Psychological Exposition for Upbuilding and Awakening*. Translated and edited by Howard V. Hong and Edna H. Hong. Princeton University Press, 1980.

Mandela, Nelson. *Long Walk to Freedom: The Autobiography of Nelson Mandela*. Little, Brown, 1994.

McCormack, Bruce L. "Grace and Being: The Role of God's Gracious Election in Karl Barth's Theological Ontology." In *The Cambridge Companion to Karl Barth*, edited by John Webster. Cambridge University Press, 2000.

McRae, Jensen. "Immune." Written by Rahki and Jensen McRae. Human Re Sources, 2021.

Melo, Yanan. "Black Body and Blood: The Eucharistic Imagination of Racial Capitalism (and How the Earth Groans in Defiance)." Presented at the Afterlives of Slavery Conference in Washington, DC, October 19, 2023.

Moore, Marianne. *The Poems of Marianne Moore*. Edited by Grace Schulman. Penguin Press, 2005.

O'Donovan, Oliver. *The Desire of the Nations: Rediscovering the Roots of Political Theology*. Cambridge University Press, 1996.

———. *The Disappearance of Ethics: The Gifford Lectures*. Eerdmans, 2024.

———. *Entering into Rest: Theology as Ethics*. Vol. 3. Eerdmans, 2017.

———. "Good, Doing Good, and the Goods." YouTube, April 16, 2021. Presented to the Henry Center at Trinity Evangelical University. https://tinyurl.com/y2b5trnb.

———. "'Usus' and 'Fruitio' in Augustine, 'De Doctrina Christiana I.'" *Journal of Theological Studies*, n.s., 33, pt. 2 (October 1982): 361–97.

"Our Epidemic of Loneliness and Isolation." U.S. Surgeon General's Advisory on the Healing Effects of Social Connection and Community, 2023. https://tinyurl.com/46j626r3.

Patel, Eboo. *Out of Many Faiths: Religious Diversity and the American Promise*. Princeton University Press, 2018.

Peterman, Amar D. "Can Christians End Our Quest for Control?" *Sojourners*, June 2025. https://tinyurl.com/5h6pufjt.

———. "The Great American Potluck." *Sojourners*, October 11, 2021. https://tinyurl.com/335vsaz5.

———. "A Lived Theology of Belonging." In *Awake, Emerging, and Connected Meditations on Justice from a Missing Generation*, edited by Victoria Turner. SCM Press, 2024.

———. "There's No Such Thing as Colorblind Christianity." *Sojourners*, August 18, 2021. https://tinyurl.com/4t8afzem.

Peterson, Eugene. *Christ Plays in Ten Thousand Places: A Conversation in Spiritual Theology*. Eerdmans, 2008.

———. *The Jesus Way: A Conversation on the Ways That Jesus Is the Way*. Eerdmans, 2011.

Pohl, Christine D. *Making Room: Recovering Hospitality as a Christian Tradition*. Twenty-fifth anniversary ed. Eerdmans, 2024.

Rah, Soong-Chan. *Prophetic Lament: A Call for Justice in Troubled Times*. InterVarsity Press, 2015.

Rambo, Shelly. *Resurrecting Wounds: Living in the Afterlife of Trauma*. Baylor University Press, 2017.

Reichel, Hanna. *After Method: Queer Grace, Conceptual Design, and the Possibility of Theology*. Westminster John Knox, 2023.

Ricoeur, Paul. *Lectures on Imagination*. University of Chicago Press, 2024.

Rosa, Hartmut. *Democracy Needs Religion*. Translated by Valentine A. Pakis. Polity, 2024.

———. *Resonance: A Sociology of Our Relationship to the World*. Translated by James C. Wagner. Polity, 2019.

Schleiermacher, Friedrich. *On Religion: Speeches to Its Cultured Despisers*. Edited by Richard Crouter. 2nd ed. Cambridge University Press, 1996.

Smith, James K. A. *Desiring the Kingdom: Worship, Worldview, and Cultural Formation*. Brazos, 2009.

———. *How to Inhabit Time: Understanding the Past, Facing the Future, Living Faithfully* Now. Baker Books, 2022.

———. *Who's Afraid of Relativism: Community, Contingency, and Creaturehood*. Baker Academic, 2014.

———. *You Are What You Love: The Spiritual Power of Habit*. Brazos, 2016.

Stout, Jeffrey. *Democracy and Tradition*. Princeton University Press, 2005.

Taylor, Charles. *Sources of the Self: The Making of the Modern Identity*. Cambridge University Press, 1989.

Thatamanil, John J. *Circling the Elephant: A Comparative Theology of Religious Diversity*. Fordham University Press, 2020.

Thomas, Joash P. *The Justice of Jesus: Reimagining Your Church's Life Together to Pursue Liberation and Wholeness*. Brazos, 2025.

Tutu, Desmond Mpilo. *No Future Without Forgiveness*. Doubleday, 1999.

Uddin, Asma. *The Politics of Vulnerability: How to Heal Muslim-Christian Relations in a Post-Christian America*. Pegasus Books, 2021.

Varma, Ashish. "Jews and Gentiles Together in Christ? The Jerusalem Council on Racial Reconciliation." *Ex Auditu* 33 (2017).

Volf, Miroslav, Matthew Croasmun, and Ryan McAnnally-Linz. *Life Worth Living: A Guide to What Matters Most*. Open Field, 2023.

Ward, Benedicta, ed. *The Desert Fathers: Sayings of the Early Christian Monks*. Penguin Books, 2003.

Wear, Michael. *The Spirit of Our Politics: Spiritual Formation and the Renovation of Public Life*. Zondervan, 2024.

West, John. *Lessons and Carols: A Meditation on Recovery*. Eerdmans, 2023.

Wiman, Christian. *He Held Radical Light: The Art of Faith, the Faith of Art*. Farrar, Straus & Giroux, 2018.

———. *My Bright Abyss: Meditation of a Modern Believer*. Farrar, Straus & Giroux, 2013.

———. *Zero at the Bone: Fifty Entries Against Despair*. Farrar, Straus & Giroux, 2023.

Wirzba, Norman. *Food and Faith: A Theology of Eating*. 2nd ed. Cambridge University Press, 2019.

———. *Love's Braided Dance: Hope in a Time of Crisis*. Yale University Press, 2024.

———. *This Sacred Life: Humanity's Place in a Wounded World*. Cambridge University Press, 2021.

Wittgenstein, Ludwig. *Philosophical Investigations.* Translated by G. E. M. Anscombe. Blackwell, 1958.

Wolterstorff, Nicholas. *Justice: Rights and Wrongs*. Princeton University Press, 2010.

Zizioulas, John D. *Being as Communion: Studies in Personhood and the Church.* St. Vladimir's Seminary Press, 1985.

INDEX OF SUBJECTS

INDEX OF SCRIPTURE